Alan Bennett:
In a Manner of Speaking

Daphne Turner is a senior lecturer at Kingston University. She has
published on Auden in *Literature and Theology* and in *Platonism
and the English Imagination* (Cambridge University Press, 1994).

by Alan Bennett

plays
ALAN BENNETT: PLAYS ONE
(FORTY YEARS ON, GETTING ON, HABEAS CORPUS, ENJOY)
THE OLD COUNTRY
OFFICE SUITE
TWO KAFKA PLAYS
(KAFKA'S DICK, THE INSURANCE MAN)
SINGLE SPIES
(AN ENGLISHMAN ABROAD, A QUESTION OF ATTRIBUTION)
THE WIND IN THE WILLOWS
THE MADNESS OF GEORGE III

television plays
THE WRITER IN DISGUISE
OBJECTS OF AFFECTION (BBC Books)
TALKING HEADS (BBC Books)

screenplays
A PRIVATE FUNCTION
PRICK UP YOUR EARS
THE MADNESS OF KING GEORGE

autobiography
THE LADY IN THE VAN (*London Review of Books*)
WRITING HOME

Alan Bennett:
In a Manner of Speaking

DAPHNE TURNER

faber and faber
LONDON · BOSTON

First published in 1997
by Faber and Faber Limited
3 Queen Square London WC1N 3AU

Typeset by RefineCatch Limited, Bungay, Suffolk
Printed in England by Clays Ltd, St Ives plc

A CIP record for this book
is available from the British Library

ISBN 0-571-17748-4

10 9 8 7 6 5 4 3 2 1

Contents

Acknowledgements

I should like to thank Alan Bennett for allowing this book to go ahead, especially as the better I got to know his work, the more I realized how much he disliked writing about writers.

I owe an immense debt to Peter Conradi, who encouraged me to write about Bennett in the first place and gave generously of his time and advice once I had started. The cliché is precisely true: without him this book would never have been written.

Other colleagues and friends have also given generously and patiently: they have read drafts, discussed ideas, suggested improvements and helped me to prune, shape and polish. My grateful thanks go to Martin Corner, Moyna Kitchin, Jacqueline Latham, John Mepham and Frances Richardson, all of whom must often have had better things to do!

I should like to thank *Modern Drama* for permission to reprint material which first appeared in Volume XXXVII, No. 4 and which now forms the bulk of Chapters 1 and 2.

Introduction

According to 'Not History at All . . .', Alan Bennett first learned that he 'could make people laugh and liked doing it' from writing in the Suggestions Book in the Junior Common Room of his Oxford college. He started with a comic gift and a verbal talent which led to the parodies, monologues, sketches and jokes of *Beyond the Fringe* (1961–3), the revue which first made him famous, and *On the Margin* (television 1966). His first full-length play, *Forty Years On* (1968), grew from the same gifts.

The nostalgia which he managed to build into *Forty Years On* shows his wish for something more complex: to write about what he calls 'the margins of humour'. However, his first serious play was *Getting On* (1971). This was written in the tradition of English realist drama: it is a study of a person and his relationships, structured in three long scenes and played in a fixed set representing a detailed physical environment. His experience in writing jokes and comic monologues is used to characterize the central figure, a self-absorbed politician. Bennett's social concerns are beginning to emerge.

In 1972 came the breakthrough of his first television film, *A Day Out*. Like *Getting On*, it examines people in society. But Bennett found in television a medium which allowed him a far greater degree of naturalism in location and acting style, and the film showed that he had a visual as well as a verbal imagination. The intimacy and low-key approach which he found characteristic of television allowed him to write about ordinary lives in his native Yorkshire, using his native idiom. He had tried unsuccessfully to do this before when he introduced a monologue into *Beyond the Fringe* called 'The English Way of Death'.

Between 1972 and 1982 the bulk of his work was for television – the tragi-comic plays about ordinary, unexciting northern life that are widely known as Alan Bennett territory. But during this time he also wrote three stage plays which show him keeping other sides of his talent employed. In 1973 came *Habeas Corpus*, formally a traditional farce, with its jokes, the organized anarchy of a crazy plot, the cross-purposes, coincidences, trouser-dropping and mistaken identities. However, thematically it has much in common with *Sunset Across the Bay* (1975), that sad play about retirement and death in Morecambe, which was Bennett's next television play. His vision is so persistently tragi-comic that even his farce centres on the pain of the human condition. *Habeas Corpus* is a meditation on the body, and hence on ageing and mortality.

The second stage play was *The Old Country* (1977). Again, as in *Getting On*, he used the conventions of stage realism to examine a character whose personality and experience of England made him remote from anyone in the northern plays. *The Old Country* was to be the first of his three plays about the Establishment figure who becomes a spy and traitor but finds himself unable to escape from the culture that has formed him. *Enjoy* (1980) was the only stage play produced between *The Old Country* and *The Insurance Man* (1986). It has a fascinating relationship to the television plays. Like *Habeas Corpus*, it is a farce, though darker, as it starts with exactly the same situation as *Sunset Across the Bay*, and is about age and the passing of a way of life. It is also a play that reveals a deep unease about nostalgia and about re-creating the dying way of northern life for entertainment.

Soon after *Enjoy* the northern plays stopped. The last of them were broadcast in 1982. Bennett himself played the central character in *Intensive Care* and among the sequence of five plays known as *Objects of Affection* was a monologue for Patricia Routledge called 'A Woman of No Importance', on which he was to model the *Talking Heads* series in 1987.

He was to return to the north once more in 1984, with the first of his commercial films, *A Private Function*. But this time the north was not contemporary. Like *A Day Out*, this is set in the past, in 1947. He carefully avoided the nostalgia he had diagnosed in *Enjoy*. *A Private Function* is detached and satirical. For the first time, greed, selfishness, corruption, hypocrisy and contempt are stressed in northern characters and both sides of the English class divide are shown as morally corrupt. The split in England between classes had existed in Bennett's work hitherto as a split between his northern and other plays and was a subordinate interest in *A Day Out* and *The Old Country*. In *A Private Function*, the antagonism is made central. It is not an elegiac re-creation of a way of life strange to a southern audience, and Leeds in 1947 becomes a way of representing England.

In 1983, the year after the last northern television plays, the BBC broadcast *An Englishman Abroad*. Bennett had heard from Coral

Browne the story of her encounter in Moscow with Guy Burgess. In *The Old Country* Bennett had already shown interest in the upper-class spy, and was further attracted to the material because he found the situation 'funny and sad', and therefore suitable for his particular talents. *An Englishman Abroad* moved away from the understatement of the northern plays to the splendours of the British Embassy and the flourishes of Burgess's eloquence. In 1988, he was to adapt it for the stage and write a third spy play, *A Question of Attribution*, about Sir Anthony Blunt. The two were played together as a double bill, *Single Spies*.

In 1986, Bennett departed from his usual English landscapes and brought out two plays about the Czech writer, Kafka: on television, *The Insurance Man,* and on stage, *Kafka's Dick*. Much of his work since 1982 has been based on the lives of real people – Burgess, Kafka, Blunt, Joe Orton (the film *Prick Up Your Ears* (1987)) and George III (both the stage play and the film). Several of these are overtly about writers, and *A Question of Attribution* and, arguably, *An Englishman Abroad* follow up *Enjoy* by reflecting on the situation and activity of the artist.

In addition, he made three television documentaries which combine the observation of the outside world made possible by television cameras with much personal autobiographical material, opinion and reminiscence. These are *Dinner at Noon* (1988), about The Crown Hotel, Harrogate, *Portrait or Bust* (1994), about the Leeds Art Gallery, and *The Abbey*, the three programmes about Westminster Abbey (1995). All these suggest stocktaking and concern about how his personal experience and inner world relate to the outside world, a question inevitable for a writer like Bennett, who through his whole career has been an observer of behaviour, speech and places.

Alan Bennett's life has given him an insider's knowledge of the two nations into which geography and class split England. He was born in 1934 and grew up in a modest home in Leeds. His father was a butcher, and part of an extended family which Bennett wrote about affectionately in 'Uncle Clarence', an essay now published in *Writing Home*. The family made a brief, unhappy attempt to live in Guildford in 1944–5, but soon returned to Leeds. Bennett went to Oxford in 1954 as an Open Scholar in History and later worked there as a researcher and lecturer, but he did not find this congenial. After the success of *Beyond the Fringe*, he left Oxford to become a professional writer. He now has a house in Yorkshire and a house in London. Emotionally and geographically, he has kept a foot on each side of the divide. As a result, he can create the lives, assumptions and speech of people who belong to radically different social groups. His life has also made him enough of an outsider in each world to have a sharp sense of its limitations. That he makes his critique in the teeth of attachment is one aspect of his tragi-comic gift, and his constant battle with his own nostalgia is reminiscent of Philip Larkin. Bennett is not alone among writers in exploring various seductive myths about England and how they relate to the facts of experience, but his version of the relationship constructs a complex picture of what Englishness might mean.

A figure which recurs in Bennett's work is that of the southern upper-class Englishman who has become a spy: Hilary, Burgess and Blunt. They reject England while remaining archetypically English in their speech, tastes and irony, irony being, according to Bennett, a distinguishing mark of the English. Their emotional ambivalence makes these figures tragi-comic, and tragi-comedy becomes central to the version of Englishness which they represent. Bennett writes in the preface to *The Old Country* that he was often asked if Hilary was based on Kim Philby, and says that he had a different exile in mind when he wrote it: Auden. The link which this suggests between spy and writer throws light on what Bennett thinks about the writer's situation.

There is another recurring figure, generally in the television plays: a shy, incompetent, embarrassed man whose awkwardness places him on the edge of his social group. He is another sort of Englishman, lower middle-class and generally northern. Bennett calls him 'the writer in disguise'. This character embodies qualities which are also worth exploring for Bennett's picture of the writer and Englishness.

However, none of these qualities guarantees good plays. It is perhaps because Bennett is such an entertainer that he has been much underestimated as a dramatist. He is one of our wittiest writers. He is, as the director Lindsay Anderson said, good at jokes. He has an acute ear for the way people talk, and the features that mark where they come from, their social class and occupation. This gift includes a flair for parody, which he uses to protest about misuse of language. He is an ironist, comically in *A Lady of Letters*, whose respectable protagonist ends up radiantly happy in prison; more darkly in *An Englishman Abroad*, whose central figure loves what he betrays. His comic inventiveness is on a larger scale as well: witness the dazzling series of parallels in *A Question of Attribution* or the sustained misleading of the audience in *The Old Country*.

Bennett's formal inventiveness is remarkable. His work includes the modest realism of such television plays as *All Day On the Sands*; the

Talking Heads monologues, which are close to being short stories; the revue-like string of parodies which *Forty Years On* holds together; the grotesque images and surreal moments of *Enjoy* and *The Old Crowd*; the farce of *Habeas Corpus*; highly mannered, epigrammatic plays like *A Question of Attribution*; the recreation of past eras like *A Day Out*, which re-creates the pre-1914 world in nostalgic black and white film images.

He is a compassionate writer and – if *The Lady in the Van* is anything to go by – a compassionate and remarkably tolerant man. Like Larkin, he has an acute sense of the disappointment and unsatisfactory nature of ordinary life, and of the fact that people live with the foreknowledge of ageing, death, possible senility and helplessness. He has an equally acute sense of the way that contradictory desires can leave one with nowhere to settle and rest. Like Chekhov, Bennett can make one see his characters as both absurd and sad, and, like Chekhov's, Bennett's tragi-comedy is one of the reasons why his audience has such a sense of their completeness and truth.

PART ONE

Bennett's England

1   The North

'A writer is usually in two minds,' said Alan Bennett in a BBC lecture in 1992. In his own work, two landscapes occur again and again; each claiming love and loyalty; each celebrated; each mocked; each with its self-satisfied prejudices; each with its own sadness, loneliness and its own version of being cast out of paradise; each with its characteristic languages and forms of comedy. The landscape of northern England is that of the working class. To use Bennett's word, it is predominantly 'naturalistic', and its comedy arises from accurate observation of speech and behaviour. The landscape of southern England is that of privilege, of the upper middle classes and aristocracy. It is a world which has money and leisure for the graces of life, and its comedy comes from parody and the play of language and ideas. Neither landscape wins his full assent.

Bennett himself is in two minds about the North. It is limited and depressing, yet its trivia are honoured as real and the dull lives of its inhabitants are celebrated. He is also in two minds about the South. The southern landscape is seductive, but exclusive, unjust and deceptive. The landscapes are complementary as well as opposed, as they represent the different sides of the geographical, class and value lines along which England is split, seen by a writer who was born into the northern working class and who now lives as a member of the southern professional one. He has created in his plays a full picture of what 'England' means and the complex state of his love for and loyalties to it. His northern landscape emerges from an overview of the northern plays, especially of *A Day Out* and *Enjoy*, and we shall see two corresponding versions of the south: the first, affectionate and gently mocking, in *Forty Years On*; the second, much more critical, in *The Old Country*.

The northern landscape belongs mainly to his television plays. They use the northern speech which Bennett grew up with and were shot on location, so they are visibly set in real places. The southern landscape is that of plays written for the stage, which are more highly coloured and dependent on an audience's ability to create a landscape imaginatively.

But both are landscapes of the mind with which Bennett associates particular values and feelings.

The television plays are set in Lancashire and Yorkshire – Morecambe, Leeds, Halifax, Scarborough. If, as in *One Fine Day*, a play is set in London, the places we hear about are Acton, Cricklewood, Tottenham and Harlesden, not places where Sir Anthony Blunt or the headmaster of *Forty Years On* would be likely to live.

In these places the characters live in small, ordinary houses: back-to-back, terraced or semi-detached. They work for the council, in offices and factories. They may be unemployed, or pensioners in church halls, social clubs or geriatric homes. They visit launderettes, men's clubs with snooker rooms, the back room of a small shop. They travel by bus. For holidays, they choose a caravan at Skipsea, a boarding house in Morecambe or a bus tour.

Education in these plays is offered at the local comprehensive school. Although the headmaster in *Intensive Care* has some comic features in common with the headmaster of *Forty Years On*, he has no spare staff to fill up gaps on the timetable when a teacher has a family emergency. There is no mention of public schools or Oxbridge. Hopkins in *Me, I'm Afraid of Virginia Woolf* teaches English at the Polytechnic (where, as his mother complains, 'they think you teach woodwork').

Health care comes on the NHS, not by way of Harley Street. Hopkins discovers that an 'outpatients' in Halifax is not the best place to read Virginia Woolf'. The hospital in *Afternoon Off* is inadequately staffed and the staff nurse speaks a broad West Indian English that the hero cannot understand. There is nowhere comfortable for the families of patients in *Intensive Care* to spend the night.

The Chinese waiter's hotel dining room in *Afternoon Off* seems adequate, but many of Bennett's people eat less satisfactorily. The cafeteria in *Me, I'm Afraid of Virginia Woolf* has a cracked cup and a dirty sauce bottle; the food in the boarding house in *All Day on the Sands*, for all its pretensions, is rationed, monotonous, and the grapefruit segments are certainly tinned. There is a chip in the sugar, which offends Graham in the monologue of that name.

We hear a great deal about lavatories in the plays. Characters are continually using public ones: in the boarding house, at the office, in the hospital (which, according to Aunt Kitty, is 'nothing to write home about'), in the street – vandalized in *Me, I'm Afraid of Virginia Woolf*. There is no mention of private lavatories in private houses, which are desirable since we all prefer privacy in these matters: as the mother in

All Day on the Sands says, 'I'll wait a minute. I never like to see who's been in before me.'

Finally, the landscape can be squalid. There are frequent graffiti, demolition, dustbins and cardboard boxes piled up in forecourts, litter, dilapidation, a view of TV aerials and the backs of houses, and sewage pipes running out into the sea.

Bennett's northern characters are mainly lower middle and working class. A divide between privileged and unprivileged is basic between the landscapes of south and north.

His north is an intensely respectable world, conservative in dress and moral attitudes, often peopled by characters much older than Bennett. Small refinements are important, and to be 'common' is the crime, as it was in Bennett's own childhood. Leonard in *A Chip in the Sugar* is had up for exposing himself in the doorway of Sainsbury's. 'Tesco, you could understand it', says Graham's mother, assuming a distinction between refined and common.

It is a world of small snobberies and shames and social awkwardness. The family in *All Day on the Sands* cannot admit to being unemployed. Hopkins in the doctor's surgery worries: 'there were now so many empty seats that if he went on sitting there the girl would think he wanted to sit next to her. But if he sat somewhere else she would think he didn't. Life, it seemed to Hopkins, was full of such problems and literature was not much help.'

In these plays, landscape and dialogue are the work of a realist dramatist. Bennett is interested, as he says in the introduction to *Office Suite* and in his BBC television lecture in 1992, in the humdrum and in ordinary people and their speech. But it is also and necessarily a landscape of the imagination. The title of *Sunset Across the Bay* is clearly metaphorical as well as literal, in view of the story. It is about an urban couple who retire at the time when their home is about to be demolished. They buy a flat in Morecambe, where they have spent holidays in the past, and retire there – to purposelessness, loneliness, and eventually death. The real and commonplace landscape of Morecambe Bay is a poetic one as well, and the film ends with a shot of the widow walking alone over the sands. In *All Day on the Sands*, the sea is a 'distant glitter' beyond the shabby landscape of 'television aerials and the backs of boarding houses'. The family have come to the boarding house on holiday, hoping for happiness, but all through the play it remains as distant from them as that distant glitter of the sea.

This is an impoverished landscape. The people are not homeless or short of food. They have houses, education and a health service, but the facilities are minimal. The material meanness of their world echoes emotional loneliness and disappointment. Bored and lonely characters are among Bennett's preoccupations: *A Woman of no Importance*; *A Lady of Letters*; the pensioners who go to social clubs; the 'single ladies. Widows. Sad men' who go to Hopkins's evening class; the Chinese waiter of *Afternoon Off*, further isolated by his minimal English, who cries when his long search for a (finally very unpleasant) girl fails. Even people with families and partners are lonely, as they seldom experience excitement or warmth or satisfaction. Having a partner does not prevent the couple in *Sunset Across the Bay* – especially the retired man – from suffering appalling loneliness and emptiness, in which there is nothing to do but wait for death.

Living is felt to happen elsewhere, and sexual awkwardness and failure are related to feelings that one hasn't lived. When, in *Intensive Care*, Midgley of the dull teaching job and the unsatisfactory marriage goes to bed with the night nurse, he says, 'It's what people call living, is this. We're living. (*They kiss.*) I ought to have done more of this.' Hopkins, yearning for 'temporary membership of the human race', cries 'O my pale life'. His inadequacies are mirrored both in the places where he works and eats, and in his emotional relationships with his mother and girlfriend, both comical, and both awful.

In Bennett's northern landscape, life is lived with the certainty of death. It includes many hospitals (for example, *Intensive Care*, where Midgley's father dies during his son's brief moment of 'living') and old people's homes (*Rolling Home*). He also reminds us of impermanence and transience as we pass through the long corridors of hospitals and school and see or hear of many demolished buildings. Together with the buildings, apparently secure family units and neighbourhoods are also demolished. Bennett writes of filming in a demolished part of Leeds: '. . . the frontier of devastation where demolition laps at the neat front doors . . . lives now narrowed and attenuated by this approaching tide of destruction', making it quite clear that for him this real landscape has emotional and moral significance.

Technically, a play like *All Day on the Sands* offers very few of the features that grab interest in drama. The characters are fairly inarticulate and talk in cliché much of the time. It has no story to speak of. The play tells of a family's day while they are on holiday in a boarding house at Morecambe. They get up, have breakfast, spend the day on the beach and promenade and go back to the boarding house. The only narrative thread, which is conventionally started at the beginning and resolved at the end, is a very slender one. The boy, early awake and bored, drops his sister's sandal out of the window on to the flat roof underneath. During the day he steals another boy's fishing line to hook it up again. He gets into trouble. At the end the sandal is recovered. This narrative takes up less than half the play. Most of it is a series of little inconsequential exchanges. These build up a picture of the place and the kind of people in it, but any one of them could be omitted and replaced by another.

These exchanges usually have downbeat endings. For example, Part One ends like this, and is done 'very slowly with lots of gaps':

MAM: Dad.
DAD: What?
MAM: Was it tomato, them sandwiches we had at Rhyl?
DAD: When?
MAM: We had some right nice sandwiches once. Just after we were married. At Rhyl. Were they tomato?
DAD: I don't know.
MAM: I don't know either.

This is not vivid or impressive. The passage is not organized to make a point or create a climax. Instead, the act trails away in trivial subject matter, abandoning the subject because neither character knows about it. Moreover, Dad is not interested. He is half asleep and not paying attention. Is even Mam interested? The tomato sandwich has clearly crossed her mind but we don't know why. Maybe it is because their previous exchange was about food; maybe because she remembers another day on a beach. We don't know whether she cares or whether she is just chuntering on, making speech for the sake of human contact rather than meaning. This is in total contrast to the big moments at the end of both parts of *Forty Years On*, when language is used to state, to move, to play, to dazzle. Yet it is funny because it is so surprising to find this undramatic 'dramatic' moment and because the absurdity is so recognizably human. Television rather than stage is a good medium for *All Day on the Sands* as film moves in smaller units than theatre and is less emphatic. Here we can see Bennett using television to attend to the trivia of unnoticed lives, and to do more than that: we can see him turning the northern landscape with figures, which can sound boring and depressing, into something that is comic without being patronizing.

Moreover, Bennett finds ordinary people and banal situations interesting. He has always liked entertainment like music hall, which uses demotic speech, and sees this as lying behind what he writes for television himself. 'Accuracy of dialogue and precision of observation' he said in his BBC television lecture, 'do half a comic writer's job for him.' But the northern speech is not only comic. Bennett honours it by attending to it so lovingly and making it betray depth of feeling. He said that *All Day on the Sands* was about people being 'cross because they're not happy'. This family holiday is an everyday version of a root cause of human suffering: being 'cast out of Paradise' and wanting compensation, which is how the doctor in *The Insurance Man* diagnoses what is wrong with the human race – a diagnosis to which both northern and southern landscapes contribute, each in its own way.

Midgley in *Intensive Care* looks like a stereotype: sexually repressed, guilt-ridden, unsuccessful in his relationships and stuck in a dull job. But he is not stuck in this stereotype. Bennett allows him to amaze us when he says to the nice night nurse, 'What would you say if I asked you to go to bed?' For all the cautious wording, he asks for what he wants. Further, she does not rebuff him. The man has some attraction. Finally, he surprises us when he gets to bed with her: he is not shy or embarrassed, but has enough capacity for sexual joy to be happy, and free enough to 'talk rubbish in bed'. ('Not', he adds sadly and comically, 'that we do. Mrs Midgley and me.') The play is about his determination to do the proper thing by his father and be with him when he dies. The father dies while he is in bed with the nurse, and the play ends with him experiencing guilt and failure once again. These are given weight by being the play's end and ironic climax, but they do not outweigh the audience's pleasure at his moment of happiness.

So if Bennett's landscape is one of ordinary, disappointing life, people have endurance and resilience and there are small celebrations. The lady of letters ends up in jail, where she is 'radiant', busy, acquires skills (including 'the rudiments' of sexual knowledge, just in case), makes friends and is able to put her letter writing to constructive use. The alcoholic Susan in *Bed Among the Lentils* takes a lover and then loses him, but for the first time she does 'really understand what all the fuss is about' sex, and tackles her alcoholism. Hopkins at the end of *Me, I'm Afraid of Virginia Woolf* is about to start a love affair with the cheerful and independent Skinner. Interestingly, these small victories are often represented as sexual ones.

A Day Out

Bennett's first version of the north was *A Day Out*, which was televised in 1972 and which is also his first film. Made in black and white, it recreates a period: a Sunday in 1911 on which a cycling club of eleven men from a northern mill town spend a day in the country. Nothing much happens, but in the film Bennett creates a version of England, a pastoral of the north, just as in *Forty Years On* he represents England as a pastoral of the south, a way of life which is briefly glimpsed in one episode in *A Day Out*. Like the southern pastoral, the northern one is affectionately, nostalgically and comically presented, and it too is questioned as incomplete and shown to have been destroyed by the 1914–18 war. 'Never such innocence again', to quote Larkin's 'MCMXIV'.

The film simply follows the Halifax cycling club during their outing on Sunday 17th May 1911. We see them gather at eight o'clock by the War Memorial, reach a monastic ruin where they eat their picnic lunches and spend the afternoon and, more briefly, ride home in the evening. It ends with a short and wordless episode when four of the cyclists gather at the War Memorial again on November 11th 1919.

A film like this depends, more than anything sensational, on the writer's power of invention: his capacity to find things that will interest the audience in what they see and in what the characters do and say, and his capacity to handle form so that some controlling themes emerge. It starts with the title and date superimposed on shots of the town's mills, which establishes the period. The mills look large, impersonal and grim, and their gates are shut. However, they are shot in a misty light while music plays and so are seen through a softening haze that suggests nostalgia.

Bennett then begins to collect the club members. His unobtrusive inventiveness shows in the varied ways that he tracks each of the eleven men. The first four leave their very different homes with their bicycles, which provides viewers with a way of connecting them. One oversleeps and has to catch up; two come together; a father and a 'simple' son arrive on a tandem; one joins the group later as it passes his house. As they leave the town, there are shots of steep cobbled streets, narrow ginnells, stone archways, walls and bridges. It is dark and rather oppressive.

Then comes the contrast of their journey through the country. There are shots of them in silhouette on an open skyline and in a misty rural landscape, going through a wood and along a grassy track. They stop for a drink at a pub, and take a short cut through a field of cows. Finally, they arrive at 'journey's end', Fountains Abbey.

Here they spend an idyllically uneventful afternoon. They eat their lunches; some wander round the ruins with a guide book; some play cricket; they chat and tease each other; one finds a girl to pick up; one tries to feed a squirrel; they are startled by sudden shots from a gamekeeper killing rooks. The most developed episode is when Cross wanders off and stumbles into the garden of a manor house, where the fifteen-year-old daughter, Florence, asks him to tea, to her mother's implied disapproval. Her brothers arrive. He is uncomfortable and refuses their invitation to play croquet and leaves silently while they are playing.

When the men start on the journey home, the camera cuts between them and Florence setting off on horseback before waiting by the side of the road, presumably to intercept Cross. However, they are delayed. Shuttleworth feels ill and has a blackout. After a shot of the manor in the evening as the lights go on, Florence gives up and turns back home. There are final shots of them cycling through the landscape, again in silhouette, with music, an idyllic end to the day.

Then the film cuts back to the War Memorial, with the date November 11th 1919 superimposed on it. Four of the eleven cyclists, all looking much older, join in singing a hymn and then look at a wreath which carries the cycling club badge. The camera holds the Memorial as the credits roll.

Can one call the film a version of England? Bennett makes his group represent a wide range of age, background and experience, all held together in the community that is the club. They range in age from the young Cross and Appleton to Mr Shuttleworth, who is now maybe too old for these long expeditions. They include a father and son. There is a range of social class and wealth: the printed text says that Cross's father is a doctor while the film shows a large house on the outskirts of the town, with an elaborate formal garden and driveway shot from above. Shuttleworth has a prosperous shop. A cut from one to the other shows that Shorter's clock is much more elaborate and expensive than Ackroyd's. Shorter unwraps a new suit. Gibson's poverty is suggested by his eagerness to eat Baldring's apple skin and core and by his 'two scrutty little sandwiches'. The group includes the respectable and the 'common', according to Bennett the primary lines along which his mother classified people: Wilkins worries about what his church will say about his absence and whether they will get into trouble for playing cricket in the Abbey ruins; Shorter thinks the cows have left the field in 'a disgusting state'; Ackroyd is 'temperance'. But Edgar and Gibson make coarse jokes about putting 'lead in your pencil' and 'Bum before wicket'. Gibson mocks Ernest cruelly; Edgar has a crude sexual encounter. Intellectually, they range from Cross, who reads H. G. Wells, and Ackroyd, who wanders round the ruins with a guide book, has a fund of general knowledge and a keen interest in nature (he has a butterfly net, keeps rabbits and coaxes a squirrel to feed), to Ernest, the 'idiot' who makes only incoherent noises. Finally, they range politically from Boothroyd, who is a socialist and calls giving a piece of cake to Gibson 'paternalism', to the conservative Shorter, who calls it 'generosity'. It is surprising that Gibson is accepted as a member of the club and Edgar's sexual behaviour is tolerated, but they are both included in this widely varied community. The notable absence is anyone from the upper class.

What is clear to the viewer about the society shown in the film is that everyone has a place and knows it. Even on their holiday together, the hierarchical structure remains. Shuttleworth is the 'father', the founder and leader of the club. He reads the map, selects the route and the short cuts and is the final arbiter about whether to leave or wait for Edgar. Shorter is his second-in-command. They preserve the formalities of address and call each other 'Mr', though Shuttleworth calls the younger ones 'lads' and Ackroyd by his first name. With elaborate politeness he offers to buy drinks for them all: 'I hope you'll allow me to do the honours.' There is no visible resentment of this structure, even from Boothroyd and Cross. The security it offers people shows in the difference between Shuttleworth's collapse in the middle of a group which looks after him and Dad's in *Sunset Across the Bay*, alone in a public lavatory. Male companionship, which Dad misses so much, is one of its strengths.

Between the northern characters, small social differences are carefully maintained. Between all of them and the aristocracy an impassable gulf yawns. Bennett makes Cross, from the prosperous, middle-class, professional home, the character who stumbles into the manor house grounds. But even he cannot live up to his name and cross comfortably into their company. His voice marks him clearly as one of the northern group. He demonstrates his assumption that he does not belong by leaving the croquet game voluntarily. Florence's family see her as strange for wanting to establish contact with him. Her brother, though polite to Cross, betrays his arrogance when he calls her 'a frightful tart', and though her mother is not so blatant she clearly feels bewilderment about Florence's wish to cross social divides and remarks that Cross's surgical boot 'won't help the grass one bit'. At the end, Florence, aristocratically riding side-saddle, tries to contact Cross on his industrially produced bicycle. Her effort to make a human relationship across the class barrier fails. The south, the culture that would see itself and its language as dominant and mainstream, is included in the play, and made peripheral to the lives of the northern group.

If by 'pastoral' one means nostalgia for a lost good place represented by a life of harmony and ease in a rural landscape, then there are two versions of pastoral in the film: northern and southern. The southern one is only briefly present: the pastoral of the great house, croquet and tea on the lawn that is fully developed in *Forty Years On*. *A Day Out* concentrates on the pastoral of the north. 1911 was a period when northern industrial towns were still close enough to the country for it to be easily accessible. The cycling club from the mill town still sees England as rural: 'It'll be a long time before they build up England', says Boothroyd as they look down on their town and Ackroyd reflects on how much country has been built over and replaced by 'soot and smoke and streets and streets'. Indeed, this 1911 landscape persisted, according to Bennett: 'Ten years ago,' (i.e. 1962) 'when I was last here, this area looked pretty much as the nineteenth century had left it: villages huddled round the mill in the valley bottom . . . There were cobbled streets between green fields . . .' This identification of England as rural, not urban, is a persistent myth: Boothroyd's vision of a reformed England's future is expressed in pastoral terms too. As it reforms ('Man going on from strength to strength. And it's a pretty straight road now'), it is heading 'over the hill into a great green place. You come up over the top of the hill and see it stretched out before you, the twentieth century'. The verbal imagery here repeats the visual imagery of earlier in the film. The club survey their town from a green place as Boothroyd imagines England surveying its history.

Though Bennett writes that the weather in which it was shot had prevented the film from being as much of a 'gentle Edwardian idyll' with a 'long, lyrical ending' as he had intended, this viewer anyway still saw it as idyllic. Shots linger on the characters in woods, on grass tracks, by a stream. Cows prance comically, apparently in response to Boothroyd's singing. Wilkins picks flowers while music plays. Music also plays while the camera pans over Boothroyd's voice across the garden to Baldrick happily relaxed in the earth closet. Like shepherds in pastoral, the characters eat and drink, sing and play, wear a wreath of flowers, discover nymphs by brooks and make love. There is no sign of work to be done. Bennett gives his characters 'an almost perfect day'.

That 'almost' is typical Bennett. Of course the day is not quite perfect: Edgar and his nymph have a 'sex scene . . . not a love scene'; Boothroyd cannot sing in tune; Shorter sulks when given out during the cricket game; the picnics of the better-off create envy and Shorter speaks contemptuously of Gibson's 'two scrutty little sandwiches'. Still, comic anti-pastoral like this conventionally occurs in such pastoral works as *As You Like It* and *A Midsummer Night's Dream*. Gibson's petty cruelty to the idiot Edgar and his throwing his coat over Ackroyd's squirrel disturb the perfection still more. Most of all, the film makes the viewer constantly aware of all that the pastoral has to omit. It is acknowledged to be only one version of the past.

'Never such innocence again'. The society of this film and Larkin's poem may have been innocent in accepting itself the way it was and not questioning its structure and values. It is also innocent in that the audience can project on to it a simplicity that we could never place later in history. Boothroyd, the socialist, is innocently optimistic about history in a way that nobody could now be. Bennett and Larkin, looking back, are nostalgic for but not innocent about its innocence. Bennett is a historian and a man of the north. He builds into the film the landscape of the men's daily lives, which they pass through at the start of the film and which is stony, dark and grim. The title tells us that this is 'time out' from their normal existence: next day they will be back at work and Wilkins will be suffering from the disapproval of his chapel and his mother. The manor house episode reminds the audience of the potentially painful social split on which this apparently stable and secure way of life is built. Above all, there is the shocking contrast between Boothroyd's optimistic vision of twentieth century England and our knowledge of its history. The way of life shown in the film is doomed.

This is a pastoral elegy, as is *Forty Years On*, for the end of a myth and the end of a way of life. Intimations of age and death are included when Shuttleworth collapses; he is reminded that he is now 'too old to be bikin' about'. Like Dad's in *Sunset Across the Bay*, his collapse represents the end of an old way of life, though the two claim, with identical stoicism, to be 'all right'. Above all, Bennett's introduction makes it clear that he intended 'intimations of the war to come'. Boothroyd's hopes for the future are not only constantly undercut by our knowledge but also by being ironically juxtaposed to the shock of sudden shots as the gamekeeper kills rooks. The final film image of the manor house is in darkening light: Florence's brothers are part of the generation of young aristocrats killed in the war which Bennett elegized in *Forty Years On*. The directions for the original final scene run: 'The last shot is of them going over the edge of the hill back into the abyss again.' Bennett sees this shot in metaphorical terms: the abyss may suggest their daily lives, but the language could also be used of troops in the trenches. That the war destroyed seven of the eleven men is made clear in the final scene at the War Memorial. The good place has been lost and only Shuttleworth, Shorter, Wilkins and Cross are alive eight years after their day out.

So Bennett's north in *A Day Out* is gentle, apparently secure and, though industrialized, still in touch with an idyllic countryside. This version of the north is recognized as incomplete, but its loss is mourned. Bennett's ambivalence to the north shows much more harshly in *Enjoy*.

Enjoy

Enjoy is a play written not for television but for the stage. It starts with a situation very like that of the moving television play, *Sunset Across the Bay*. An elderly couple, Mam and Dad, live in a back-to-back house in Leeds. Theirs is almost the last street to survive. Their house will soon be destroyed, and they are waiting to move into a modern mais-onette. Like the husband in *Sunset Across the Bay*, Dad once had six men under him. They share preoccupations found in other northern plays: the concern with being 'refined' and with 'toilets'. As in *Sunset Across the Bay* and *A Day Out*, a way of life is dying: '. . . the disappear-ing world. Leeds. Bradford. Halifax. A way of life on its last legs'. Mam is losing her memory; Dad starts disabled and ends paralysed.

But where the other two plays are elegiac and compassionate, *Enjoy* is a dark and fantastic comedy and much more scathing about the northern way of life. The Council are afraid of destroying valuable elements in traditional communities, so they send a sociologist to be a silent observer of Mam and Dad. Later, two other characters arrive, both with their observers in tow. Ms Craig, the sociologist attached to Mam and Dad, turns out to be a man in women's clothes, and is later discovered to be their long-lost son. Ms Craig plans that her parents and their home should be moved to a theme-park that will re-create the old community. Mam eventually moves, but Dad, paralysed and incontinent, ends in hospital. The doubling and trebling of the silent observers make a point by comic exaggeration; the sociologist in drag is a comic fantasy; there are standard comic conventions like the recog-nition of the long-lost child in such plays as *The Winter's Tale* and *The Marriage of Figaro*, or the resurrection of somebody who has been taken for dead and laid out in *The Shadow of the Glen* and *The Caucasian Chalk Circle*. There are moments which remind us of Pinter's comedy, when his characters make surreal, inexplicable and disturbing shifts of language-register: Mam and Dad occasionally make similar shifts from their normal northern speech to the language of journalism. There is a parody of D. H. Lawrence.

These kinds of comic fantasy prevent sympathetic identification with the characters. Further, darker characteristics emerge than in Bennett's other northern plays. Mam blames Dad for her narrow life: she could have been another Kathleen Ferrier. Dad is unpleasant and sunk in much more damaging fantasy. He looks at pornography, has 'interfered with' his daughter and rejected his transvestite son. There is a moment when he uses sexual fantasy to attack the sociologist. Later, he offers to give his prostitute daughter's clients a kick by acting as voyeur. It is small wonder that both children have escaped from this cramped and squalid place, Linda into prostitution, consumer goods and fantasies of travel, their son into something else. All this suggests *Enjoy* as a play that rejects the north.

But Ms Craig has not exactly rejected the north. She returns to it and wants to re-create it as a theme-park. *Enjoy* is a play soaked in nostalgia from the moment when it opens with the first of Mam's many Ivor Novello songs. The theme is first stated as received wisdom in sociological terms: the Council is anxious not to ignore the value of the social structure in the city's traditional communities. Another version of the theme is given as the climax of Act 1. Ms Craig has been present, but silent, for more than half the act. It is a release and satisfaction when she is left alone and finally speaks. She looks at the mantelpiece and names all the articles which have accumulated there. She comments that it is 'a shrine laden with the relics of the recent past and a testimonial to the faith that one day the world will turn and the past come back into its own and there will be a restoration'. This is the intelligent observer, drawing conclusions, generalizing and voicing a theme of the play. The speech continues with the elegiac longing for the past to be restored, figurative ('On that day the nasturtiums will be planted'), comic ('the skin complaint will recur and the ointment be applied once more'), and formally shaped, a set piece. (It ends, as it opens, with the clock.) The act ends, as Mam and Dad re-enter, with another Novello song.

The climax of the play at the end of Act 2 is when Ms Craig's plans for restoring the past are revealed. She is the initiator; the plan satisfies her imaginative need. All will be as 'when I was little'. It will be done 'for love'. Mam is delighted. Dad is dubious, but when threatened with exclusion he announces, 'I want to be preserved too.' 'Preserved' suggests that this way of life, however desired, is doomed and anachronistic now.

So, in the play, there is the double pull of nostalgia for a way of life and the rejection of it. There is also Bennett's judgement on this nostalgia for the north. He mocks the Council's desire to preserve the past by the absurd device of three observers following three characters, notebooks at the ready. The choral voice with which Ms Craig first speaks is undermined when we learn that she is manipulating the situation for her own ends, and, at the very end, that her home is also a nostalgically preserved bit of the past – a 'done up' farmhouse in 'another world', forty minutes away where Leeds is sentimentally 'a glow in the sky'.

The comic attack on nostalgia is broadest when Dad supposedly has died and Mrs Clegg comes in to assist Mam. She acts as a 'tower of strength' to show her observer that she is part of a traditional neighbourly community. She is determined to do the traditional thing, insisting that she and Mam wash and lay out the body themselves. There follows a parody of D. H. Lawrence's *The Widowing of Mrs Holroyd*, which Bennett saw at the Royal Court in the 1970s, and in which a wife and mother wash and lay out the body of the victim of a mine accident. In *Enjoy*, Mam, washing Dad's body, causes him to have an erection, a turn of events, Bennett writes, that took him as much by surprise as it did Mam. The attack on nostalgia darkens when Ms Craig's team arrive and completely ignore the people they are claiming to protect and preserve: 'Get a sample of that wallpaper. It's terrible . . . I like the bath. The bath comes over loud and clear.'

Bennett seems here to be uneasy that his northern plays may distort their material by vulgar sentimentalizing: the theme-park will carefully and expensively re-create the poverty of northern life for entertainment. He suggests here that the northern landscape he has created in so many plays is as fake as the southern landscape that Hilary in *The Old Country* creates in Russia. Indeed, only two years after *Enjoy* (1980) he wrote *Intensive Care* (1982), the last of his northern plays.

2   The South

Forty Years On

Bennett's plays are not confined to a northern setting. He has also
created a southern one, diametrically its opposite, and *Forty Years On*
is the first and simplest version of it. It calls itself England – though it is
not, since it is the landscape of only part of England: 'Berkshire and
Hampshire, Leicestershire and Rutland', excluding the north. It is only
one of the possible versions of the south – because it is the landscape of
power and privilege.

When its inhabitants are in cities, they are in London, in Hampstead
and St John's Wood, rather than Acton. They dine at Simpsons and take
refuge from the war in Claridges. They sit on Royal Commissions and
the Board of Covent Garden, visit palaces and work in prestigious
institutions like the Foreign Office and the Courtauld Institute, with its
fine furniture and paintings. Their suits are made to measure and their
pyjamas come from the firm which supplies the royal family. They
have nannies and nurseries, and go to public schools, in one of which
Forty Years On is set. They belong to the Church of England, and sing
its hymns long after belief has departed. Sometimes they are philistines,
like the headmaster in *Forty Years On* but, when they have taste, like
Duff in *The Old Country*, what they admire becomes mainstream culture. They have an unassailable assurance, which they casually take for
granted: a 'careless grace, bred out of money', says Tempest. In *Getting
On*, George longs for his suit to look like that of 'Sir Kenneth Clark . . .
or the head of an Oxford College', but he knows it never will, because
he does not have the unselfconscious assurance to transmit to it. There
is practically no mention of the essentials of living which dominate the
northern plays – food, sanitation, hospitals. This is a landscape of the
privileged, where all amenities are taken for granted and from which
the plebeians are excluded. In every way, it is the opposite of the
northern landscape.

Neither is it an exclusively urban landscape. It involves London, but
is also the world of the great house and the peaceful green countryside

of the home counties. The big house is remembered by Hilary in *The Old Country*, and is seen in *A Day Out*. However, Bennett's main tribute to the ideal of the great house comes in *Forty Years On*, in the story of the night-time visit to Kimber, an imaginary house set, like Knole, in Kent. It forms the climax of Act One. A group of young aristocrats go to Kimber on an August evening in 1914; these include Julian Grenfell, soon to be killed. They go to hear the nightingales, with all their associations with beauty, enchantment and longing, from Keats and other English poets. Kimber is locked and shuttered, but the young insiders know how to enter it and, as they do, they enter the enchanted place of childhood. Moonlight, the magical light of *A Midsummer Night's Dream*, lies across the rooms. When the bell is rung, there is an elusive response ('a faint answering ring') from the deserted kitchen. The house is a labyrinth that leads back into the past, to the door 'where I had not been since I was a child'. It is a moment of such happiness that 'I could afford melancholy', a mood understood by another Romantic poet, Wordsworth. This delicious melancholy accompanies a reminder that these golden youths must die ('Our children ... such of us as survived to have them'), though the speaker imagines with sad irony that 'there would be other nights and time yet': and, as the short midsummer night ends the nightingale's song mingles with the rumble of the Flanders guns.

This is a piece of writing as deeply rooted in the English literary and Romantic tradition as Yeats's lines on another great house: 'We were the last Romantics, chose for theme / Traditional sanctity and loveliness'. It is an elegy for doomed youth and a celebration, just like Yeats's poem or Vita Sackville-West's book on Knole, of the aristocratic ideal. Why should the great house have such a grip on the English literary imagination? Bennett emphasizes the connection with childhood memories, and thus the great house becomes another version of the pastoral – Eden, the lost good place. The young men's access to Kimber is a fantasy of its recovery.

This speech is the first climax of a play which pokes fun at England's outdated picture of itself and is put into the mouth of the headmaster, whom Bennett usually undermines by making anything he utters contradictory ('I'm all in favour of free expression, provided it's kept rigidly under control') or parodic, such as his confused prayers in the cadences of Cranmer. In fact, the play was designed to hold a series of revue turns and parodies together. But this speech is pastiche, not parody. It uses stylistic clichés, but not satire and ridicule. Only when the act ends, not on the dying fall but with Matron bathetically distributing milk bottles, is there any hint that the author might not identify completely with the celebration.

This is a pastoral world: both Georgian, in its picture of England as rural, and literary, in its vocabulary and the Blake-like presence of the lambs in the city. The headmaster recalls 'proud young trees', 'a quiet English village', squire and blacksmith, 'clear dewy grass with birds singing', 'smooth green lawns' and sunshine. There are teas on the lawn and boats on the lake. Tennyson's lush 'The splendour falls on castle walls' is quoted. Ottoline Morrell and Bertrand Russell see sheep and lambs as they walk from Regents Park to Primrose Hill. It is a land in which, as in pastoral, the necessities of life do not have to be considered. Both the play *Forty Years On* itself and its southern landscape are worlds of innocence, not experience.

The first parody in the play is of *The Importance of Being Earnest*. It is a kind of Eden, in the sense that Auden defined Eden in 'Music in Shakespeare' – a 'place of pure play where suffering is unknown'. None of the characters is capable of feeling pain; our sympathy and moral judgement are not required, and watching their embarrassments gives us only delight. It is a similar literary world to that of Wilde or P. G. Wodehouse, where again there is no sin, but style is all. As a result, both of their worlds are without adult sexuality. *Forty Years On*, though it runs to schoolboys' smutty jokes, is the same.

Nostalgia, one chief feature of pastoral, is constantly present. Tempest's memory is of a 'land of lost content'. Hugh and Moggie are 'two nice people in a world we have lost'. The play starts with memory: the headmaster goes back over a lifetime at the school, and in its idiosyncratic way the play recapitulates the course of twentieth-century history. There is nostalgia for childhood in other passages than the story of Kimber. 'Visions of boyhood' are what the school song hopes will remain with the adult as 'glimpses' and 'echoes of dreamland'. Indeed, the need to retain lifelong links with the school, and, as the play does, to see school as a metaphor for the adult world is a form of nostalgia too.

The end of the play is an elegy for an England lost. This passage begins with an elegy by G. J. Whyte-Melville, while boys hum the school song under it. Then the five main characters come forward, ceasing to be the voices that have clashed through the whole play. Instead, the liberal Franklin and the conservative Head unite as voices in a chorus which stylistically owes much to T. S. Eliot's choruses from 'The Rock': images of crass modern life and 'underprivileged hearts' are used lyrically to mourn what they are not. Although the Head admits that 'romantic and old-fashioned' ideas 'didn't have much to do with justice', and the reader from the lectern wittily summarizes England's present state in estate agent's jargon, the play ends not with bathos, like Act One, but with full organ, descant and a hymn. Bennett's wit shows him to be aware of the clichés, but does not destroy the poetic devices and music which are used to move and mourn.

But however much we may enjoy this landscape, and however it tugs at the heartstrings, the vision is not viable, and Bennett knows it – this England is out of date. The war will herald the ending of the England of 'The Breed', the club celebrated by Sapper and by Buchan, whose novels, such as *The Thirty-Nine Steps*, the play parodies. The headmaster, representing the old assumptions, is about to retire and be replaced by Franklin, who intends to abolish compulsory games and corporal punishment. The headmaster sees this as the 'collapse of all I hold most dear', but accepts that change is inevitable. At the end, when he admits to the system's lack of justice, he sees the 'crowd' making its way into the secret garden of the privileged and destroying it. The delightful place is doomed. In the bleak new world, even a butterfly will be 'an event'; the combined forces of materialism and democratization will destroy the myths of both north and south and replace them with vulgar consumer capitalism. Faced with *this* force, both north *and* south are doomed to become lost worlds.

Meanwhile, the south is an absurd world, though Bennett delights in its absurdity. Parody allows a writer to have it both ways: he can love that which he mistrusts and mocks. Good parodies are possible only when a writer is soaked in the style and feeling of what he ridicules. The humour, unlike that of Hilary in *The Old Country*, is quite unaggressive. The audience is invited to join the inner circle. The more they are soaked in the cultural mainstream and can recognize the parodies and references, the more they will enjoy the play. Further, they are invited to collude by taking part in the play themselves: Bennett presses them into service as the audience of parents and has the headmaster address them as such. There are splendid parodies, and Bennett's delight in jokes and word-play is given its head: 'Related to the Woolf family through some Alsatian cousins'; 'Spontaneous? Then it must be stopped at once'; 'an unmade Bedouin of great beauty'.

If Bennett knows that the England of 1914 deserved to die and did, the Romantic tug towards it goes deep and has to be resisted. In this play, the resistance is the gentlest of satire and much fun. But there are other plays, like *The Old Country*, where the clash between Bennett's two minds is more complex and more painful.

The Old Country

The Old Country also marginalizes the north by picturing England as a southern landscape very like that of *Forty Years On*. Its London is also that of Simpsons, St Johns Wood and Hampstead; Surrey, Salisbury, Hampshire and the Scotland of grouse moors and shooting parties found in Buchan. Again, this rural landscape is where the 'great, good place' is found: 'a second Walden', says Duff, invoking pastoral as he compliments Bron on her garden. When Duff speaks of 'A country house. Wine. Talk. Friends', he sounds for a moment like Tempest describing the great house idyll in *Forty Years On*. It is the landscape of the privileged and their institutions. It is also, as in *Forty Years On*, a landscape changing for the worse in the eyes of its members. But *The Old Country* tests the southern landscape far more than *Forty Years On* does. The people are unpleasant, the wit ironic, and the moral exploration more overt. Pastoral, gently mocked in the earlier play, is here pressed to reveal its contradictions. The longed-for world is cramping and has produced its own kind of discontent and loneliness. *Forty Years On* had none of the loneliness of the north. Here, we meet the loneliness of the south. The lonely man in this play is Hilary, an upper-class man who goes into internal exile as a spy and then into literal exile in Russia. This kind of loner obviously fascinates Bennett, since *The Old Country* is the first of three plays about upper-class traitors.

The play opens with Hilary and his wife in 'a very English scene', an untidy veranda above a garden, books, a rocking chair and Elgar on the gramophone. Not until a third of the way into the play do we learn that we are in fact in Russia and that Hilary was a spy. They are visited by Duff and Veronica, and by Eric and Olga, a petit bourgeois Englishman and his foreign wife. Duff is a powerful Establishment figure, and his job is to get Hilary to agree to return to England to face whatever he must, as part of a deal between the English and Russian governments. The play ends with Hilary's reluctant departure, and Eric being left behind.

The southern landscape of *The Old Country* is much more treacherous than that in *Forty Years On*. Its pleasing surface cannot be trusted. Indeed, Bennett makes a specific connection between landscape and treachery. Hilary goes to the suburbs of Ruislip to pass on information. This is a landscape which is neither that of the southern city nor of the pastoral idyll. That particular idea of England is betrayed by it, as it is by Hilary's action. Duff says that it is the landscape of an England that has already betrayed itself. Moreover, the home counties are seen in a startling and shocking way early in the play. Hilary presses Olga (and teases the audience, who still do not know that the play is set in Russia) about the landscape outside. He asks her to suppose she was set down in it without any context for knowing where she was, and to say where she would suppose herself to be. He describes a train journey like that which so many Jews made to the death camps, and supposes the doors being opened on this landscape: 'Where would you say you were? . . . It's the common at Pirbright as seen from the Salisbury train. Or half a dozen places in Hampshire.' To an Englishman who has never had such extreme situations on his soil, this is an incongruity which is comic. But it is also terrible to be required to visualize such places in the southern landscape. A chasm opens in it through which we glimpse nightmare.

The play builds up a landscape which betrays us. The 'very English scene' of the opening is fake, a trap into which we tumble. Like a spy, it presents us with a surface that is not what it seems. 'It is a trap, this haven', says Hilary as he parodies Buchan. *Forty Years On* and *The Old Country* share this parody. In *Forty Years On* it is just fun, a revue turn. Here it is ironic and thematic. Hilary, like the hero in his Buchan parody, is in a refuge that looks English and safe. But it is treacherous, and he is going to be flushed out of it. In Hilary, as in Buchan, treachery wears an upper-class face. In several of Buchan's novels and in Bennett's parody of them, the hero is deceived into trusting a stereotypically respectable house and couple. The audience is deceived in the same way by the house and couple on the stage.

Bennett sets the trap. When Hilary says, 'Today . . . the people, God bless them, will be out in force', we think of an English Bank holiday. When he says, 'I get it every day at the office', we assume he means London. Hilary sends Bron to the phone telling her that Stalin was ringing from a Haslemere call box. We think the joke is that Russia is so alien and remote. Later, we learn that Haslemere is the incongruously distant place.

We realize that we have walked into a trap when Bron says to Hilary that he has one thing in common with Eric: 'You're all traitors' and immediately Duff and Veronica arrive in an Embassy car and announce Moscow is 'boiling'. Both the English landscape and the English gentleman are not what they seemed. Their surfaces are attractive, but beneath is treachery.

The England we hear about in *The Old Country* is much more morally corrupt than the essentially comic vision of England in *Forty Years On*, that play world in which no real harm or pain happens. Hilary's business is to expose southern values, which he does with bitter irony. But however much we may admire his intelligence, assent to his perceptions and enjoy his wit, we do not identify with him. Bron points out, as does the pyjama seller at the end of *An Englishman Abroad*, that people had died as a result of what he did: 'And not merely died. Eventually died. Good people. Friends', she says, implying torture and betrayal of trust. And it is shocking when Hilary, having described the death trains, calls Olga a 'Jewish bitch'.

If one compares Duff with the headmaster of *Forty Years On* as representative figures of the Establishment, the attack now is much more morally charged, for all Bennett's comic presentation. His continual cultural reference comes less from enjoyment than from a sensibility paraded for status and used for power. His arrogance and sense of privilege flash out when Hilary objects that he cannot return because he is a Soviet citizen: 'A technicality. To do with ordinary people' – not, by implication, with us. Ordinary people are 'Trevor, a counter assistant', presumably one of the nobodies from the northern plays. Eric is also ordinary people. We discover at the end that Duff once picked Eric up in a public lavatory and took him home for the night. Eric remembers being politely treated, but Duff now denies the episode. Brief sexual contact is all right, but a great gulf is still fixed between them.

Eric is a draughtsman from the Portsmouth Dockyards, and from his entrance Bennett insists on his sad sense of inferiority and difference. 'Our place isn't like this', he says just after he comes on stage. He knows that his manners may embarrass Bron: 'I wouldn't talk. I wouldn't show you up'. But it is more than that. The ambassador is at home in his own culture. He can take it for granted: *Horizon* is his 'parish magazine'. Eric is not at home in the culture of his own country. He is a foreigner in it, as he is in Russia. He envies Bron her simple liking for picking up bits of stone and pebbles. She can do it without self-consciousness; he would worry about his taste. Later we learn that when he goes into an art gallery he looks at the pictures he has seen in reproduction, because they 'must be the best'. He is not free just to enjoy them. Bennett's acute ear for speech makes Eric talk as upper-class characters would not. 'That's art' or 'My personal piece of sky. Heaven' are what none of the others would say, unless ironically. Eric lacks irony, which is Hilary's main mode of speech and the one Hilary identifies as most characteristically English. Eric is left behind at the end of the play, longing to go home but without the political importance to matter, clutching an armful of books he will not read which represent the culture from which he is excluded.

Olga emphasizes the Englishness of the others by being foreign and belonging to no English class. She has experienced something so 'much worse nothing else counts' – to her the 'past is simply misery and horror'. Exactly what her history is, we don't know, but since she is Jewish and objects to Hilary's story of the train journey, we may suppose that she is one of the people who experienced those extremes of suffering and political cruelty that England has been spared. As a result, she has a different sense of proportion and different values. To her the myth of England is archaic: 'These little feelings do not matter. Nice. They belong to the past.' She is not concerned with being 'nice', with Bron's indirectness and reticence or Eric's deference, because putting oneself in someone else's place are 'luxuries for which there is no time any more'. As a result she openly speaks her mind ('Your husband does not like me'), regardless of the embarrassment she causes. To her, Bron and Eric are alike: the English 'are the most embarrassed nation in the world' because they still believe in a society where the basic social contract is 'I won't make you feel bad as long as you don't make me feel bad'. She is perceptive enough to see that she makes people uncomfortable, un-English enough to say so and intelligent enough to know that to them 'it is in bad taste to say that. It is without irony'. Through her, Bennett identifies good taste as one of the south's motivating principles and irony as basic to that taste. Hilary does the same, later in the play, when he calls irony 'the English speciality'.

Parody is *Forty Years On*'s means of having it both ways – though there are good parodies in *The Old Country*, its main technical means is irony. The title is ironic: it means both a decrepit dying country and a country lost and longed for. The landscape we are presented with says 'England' but turns out to be 'Russia'. Hilary appears to be an English gentleman but is really a Soviet citizen and traitor. Irony is his chief mode of speech. Bennett recognizes it as morally dubious when Hilary, like Olga, discusses irony – ironically, of course. He recognizes it as something that the English are born to ('It's the amniotic fluid') and as a refusal to commit oneself, a way of avoiding 'guilt and purpose and responsibility'. Bennett shows, in the introduction to *Two Kafka Plays*, that he is very much aware of the irony that he is an ironic writer himself.

Hilary has rejected England. Since he is the central figure in the play, we want to know why, but it is hard to know him. He is opaque, but in a different way from Bennett's northern characters, who are less articulate. Hilary throws out a smoke-screen of ironic words which do not mean what they say – or rather, mean exactly what they say, because he intends them to mean something else. When Eric and Olga, whom he dislikes and despises, ask him out for a picnic, he explains to Bron, 'It appears our young friends are picnic-bound and we oldsters are more than welcome to tag along . . . weeks go by and nothing doing then treat jostles with treat'. Here he speaks the clichés of the kind of character he had to pretend to be and fakes the language of his own class, both using and rejecting it through irony at the same time. What Hilary is remains concealed. We have to infer it, as we did with the inarticulate northern characters. All we can see is the aggressive rejection of English manners and idiom. Here, Bron tells him not to be silly. At the end, with pain and exasperation, she says 'Oh stop it. Stop it. You've no need to keep it up now'.

The question is why he needs to keep it up at all. It is a defence against being known. Both as an English gentleman and as a spy, he had to conceal what he was. A spy is forced to be an ironist. As the play ends, Hilary is asked why he became a spy. He answers, 'the guilt of one's breeding . . . The best motives gone wrong'. But then comes the ironical avoidance: 'Would that find favour?' Pressed, he dodges into ironic reflections on the Church of England, the nursery and the family. Finally, he makes an admission: 'To be on one's own. Alone.' This is also the answer given by Bennett's other spy, Burgess. At the climax of his speech, Hilary says, 'That is what you have to do to be cast out. Murder children.'

Hilary wants to be cast out. He is a non-joiner. He feels at home only in exile and never imagined he would have to join the Russians either. He is a hare – 'swift, solitary, creatures of the open field', he says after he has shot one – not 'gregarious, slow-moving' like a rabbit. The desire to be alone and keep others excluded leads him first to the inner exile of the spy and then to actual exile. It seems that he wishes to exclude himself from the exclusive south. The landscape is too claustrophobic. He will not join the in-group, so he betrays it instead.

Yet, ironically and comically, Hilary remains English, as Burgess and Blunt do. He remains English in his irony and self-concealment. He is English in his prejudices, culture and love for the Church of England (it is the one admission of love that he makes), and he and Bron have created an English home in Russia. Like Burgess, he does not want England to change and is quite aware of the paradox. Ideologically, for England to change would be a good thing; but his 'personal inclination' would see any change as decay. Hilary, like Bennett, remains in two minds.

Finally, both north and south have a common enemy. The north of

Enjoy is a version of the north found in the television plays, but its south is not the south of *Forty Years On* and *The Old Country*. The south which Ms Craig has escaped to and whose 'consumer goods' Linda longs for is the south of modern consumer capitalism. Mam and Dad often reproduce the language of magazines, which are funded by advertising to sell goods, ('Try these easy to make prepared in advance menus and be a relaxed and carefree hostess'); of television ('You want to make it [Dad's handicap] a challenge, something to be overcome'); of newspapers ('Sweden boasts some fine modern architecture plus a free-wheeling attitude towards personal morality'); of American English ('Are you motorized?'). These moments are comic and unsettling as are some of Mick's speeches in Pinter's *The Caretaker*: they are incongruous and make us lose our linguistic bearings. The northerners in *Enjoy* are between two worlds, historically and linguistically; the southerners are going to make money from people's nostalgia by keeping their lost world artificially alive in a theme-park.

Something similar happens in Bennett's stage version of *The Wind in the Willows*. The southern pastoral landscape of the book is updated by turning Grahame's Wild Wooders into 'property speculators and estate agents', who hope to turn Toad Hall into 'Toad Hall Park and Leisure Centre'. Bennett is in two minds about both his northern and southern myths. But both are being attacked by the same enemy, which devours and transforms all traditions.

3   The Destruction of the Traditions

The Wind in the Willows

Bennett has three plays in which the two traditions of England are threatened by vulgar consumer capitalism: *The Wind in the Willows*, a children's Christmas play, *Enjoy*, a surreal play of northern life, and *A Private Function*, a satirical film comedy. Though it may seem odd to include *The Wind in the Willows* in a piece about Bennett's picture of England, the play, like *Forty Years On*, treats the pastoral myth of England with affection, yet sends it up sufficiently to generate some sense of its incompleteness, and also shows it as threatened. The particular social realities from which the threat comes may not be of central importance in this play – Bennett presents them as a joke – but it is worth noticing the characters he chose to embody the threat when his imagination was freewheeling playfully.

Forty Years On is the play closest in spirit to *The Wind in the Willows*. They both deal with the myth of a pastoral England nostalgically and playfully. In the earlier play, the myth is shown to be dying, and is both mocked and lovingly elegized. The threat to it comes from within, in the shape of Franklin, and also from without: the elegiac chorus at the end describes the secret garden as being invaded by the *hoi polloi*. This is an image of social change to which one cannot wholly object, for, as the headmaster admits, the secret garden 'didn't have much to do with justice'. *The Wind in the Willows* has much in common with this. Bennett indicates in the stage directions that its England is a place of the countryside, river, wood, field, wild animals and the seasons. It is also the England of the great house and eccentric landowner, Toad of Toad Hall. Bennett continues to make the pastoral myth explicit, as Toad and Rat identify a pastoral landscape with England: 'The chequered counties. England spread out in front of us'. In contrast to *Forty Years On*, the Eden of *The Wind in the Willows* is under threat from vulgar commercialism. The invaders are not the people that the snobbish headmaster vaguely calls the 'crowd', but are clearly identified at the climax of the play as the property speculators of the mid-eighties boom.

For the Romantics, childhood became another version of pastoral, and this particular pastoral is clearly present in both Grahame's and Bennett's work. To Wordsworth, children were in touch with natural wisdom. To psychoanalysts, adults can project their nostalgia for the lost good place on to childhood, when the relationship with the mother was unbroken. *The Wind in the Willows* is a book from which generations of English children have learned to imagine the pastoral of childhood. Grahame's pastoral includes not only the great house, but also smaller, cosier homes. Contentment with home and its suitability as a subject for the poet is claimed at the end of the chapter of the book entitled 'Wayfarers All'. In it, as in the opening sequence of *Passport to Pimlico*, the ordinary qualities of England win over those of the exotic and sunbathed south and are associated with sanity.

The Wind in the Willows is Bennett's only play which is primarily for children, and which puts children and childhood on the stage. *Forty Years On* also has children in the cast, but they are adolescent, sophisticated pseudo-adults at a public school, and the play is suitable only for an adult audience. *The Wind in the Willows* is a pastoral of childhood: the play is about holidays (it is a festive comedy, and was produced by the National Theatre as its Christmas play – a carol ends part one); the stage props are large toys (a train, a motor car, a boat), which are played with and obviously work; there are miniature houses. The characters do things that children enjoy: they go rowing on the river; have a picnic and go home to bath and bed; or go camping in a caravan. They do things that children might fantasize about – have adventures, steal cars, defy authority, escape from prison.

Mole is described as looking like a bespectacled northern schoolboy; Rat and Badger talk to him as schoolmasters or nannies might; Toad is made to wash and Mole apologizes like a deferential child and learns his lessons. Adults protect the 'child' Mole from danger and comfort 'little chaps' with hot soup. Toad has to learn to conform, and suppress some of his innocent self-centred bumptiousness. Victory is celebrated by returning Toad Hall to the neatness of the school dormitory. It is a protective environment but without visible women, perhaps like a prep school. The characters enjoy cosiness and rootedness. Mole yearns for home. Lastly, the main characters are innocent like children: not because they are free of faults but because they do not know that there is anything which needs to be changed.

So childhood, one version of the pastoral myth of England, is strongly present. However, this myth is undercut, albeit in a different way than it is in *Forty Years On*, where the main tools are the parody and pastiche of sophisticated adult literature. It is true that *The Wind in the Willows* contains parody: Bennett winks at the adult reader in the stage directions and at the adult audience when he includes in his play climactic moments from Conrad's *The Heart of Darkness* ('Oh, the horror! The horror!') and Ibsen's *Ghosts* ('Give me the sun'). But the play is an adaptation of the book, not a parody, which means that the writer has to take the myth as given, and the audience has to suspend disbelief and enter that world. In *Forty Years On*, the myth appears from the start as reminiscence coloured by the untrustworthiness of memory or feeling, and is constantly undercut by the unromantic 'real' world of Albion House. Also, in writing a children's entertainment and a comedy, Bennett needs to preserve the reassurance of the book and its affirmation that all can be made right in the end. He has to end with victory over the villains, who are expelled and made obedient. There are celebrations and a dance for the group, and a transformation of the character who is out of line.

Yet Bennett is no longer interested in writing a totally reassuring play. As he says in the introduction: 'I felt that the atmosphere of the River Bank had to be less serene'. The play undermines its own cosiness in a very delicate and finely judged way. It could be said that this is the work of an older dramatist. *Forty Years On* is enjoyable as a game, with its parodies and the Chinese boxes of its three story levels. There is subtlety and simplicity in *The Wind in the Willows*, hard won from Grahame's episodic book. There is unease in Grahame, demonstrated in the wanderlust chapter and the terror of the wild wood. But Bennett's unease comes from a greater degree of psychological realism, the presence of danger, and some uncertainty at the end, a departure from the security of Grahame's ending. Bennett's selections from the book and his departures from it are worth noticing. As he says: 'My additions and alterations . . . are . . . as revealing of me as the original text is of Grahame.'

Bennett undercuts pastoral with laughter, as he does in *Forty Years On*. His characteristically comic voice supplants Grahame's, whose manner Bennett describes as 'lyrical'. The most emotional passages are reduced. Bennett has the courage to include the Pan episode, but he sends up its style. By implication, he finds the passage 'hard to take', as he says of other work by Grahame. Bennett sandwiches the scene between Albert the horse doing his Eeyore act and the comic chase of Toad. The ecstasy is omitted, and we are left only with the music and the forgetting. In the stage directions, Bennett ironizes the sentiment for the reader: as the strange music starts and Rat says touchingly that he has never heard it before but seems to know it, the commentary runs: 'This of course is the case with lots of music but Rat, who has never been to the Wigmore Hall, is not to know that.' Bennett ironizes Toad's pastoral outburst about his caravan by exaggeration, and similarly treats the sentiment that music melts hard hearts by having the villainous weasels join in singing the campfire song. Comparing the opening section of the play with the opening chapter of the book, the shift towards comedy is clear. Grahame opens with an evocation of 'divine discontent and longing', when a mysterious 'something' calls Mole to leave his home, characterized by the repeated and sentimentalizing 'little'. This is followed by a brush with the rabbits, too short to break the lyrical mood. Bennett opens with a troop of rabbits, and the tone of the stage directions indicates that the presentation is playful: 'All the River Bank animals seem to patronize the same outfitters'. Mole's 'divine discontent' is briskly summarized in the two opening lines; the rabbit's speech that Grahame's Mole ignores is turned into skittish dialogue, with jokes and rhymes, and there is a wink at the audience – assuming they have read Beatrix Potter – when Mole teases a rabbit by calling it 'Flopsy'. The costumes are comic. The weasels spoken of in the book in a 'hesitating' and fearful way, make a brief and comic appearance in gangster outfits of 'camelhair coats, Homburg hats and co-respondent shoes'. Otter wears a 'striped Victorian bathing suit' and Portly, his baby, introduced at this point by Bennett in preparation for the 'Gates of Dawn' scene, is learning to swim, and appears wearing an 'L' plate. Later, he jumps nervously into the river, holding his nose. There are jokes in plenty: Rabbit Ronald is offended when Hedgehog Herbert says that Rat needs 'Somebody to rabbit on to', but gets his revenge in the clinching line of the scene by remarking to Herbert that Rat is 'too prickly'.

So where Grahame relies on the separate Toad story for the comedy, Bennett discovers possibilities for verbal and visual jokes and ironic commentary in other parts of the book, and the emotional temperature is much lowered.

Bennett himself views his pastoral as being made less serene by having the animals 'prey to more complicated feelings' and making them grow and change. Pastoral is static rather than dynamic, but Bennett who sees no human life as a success story, was not content with Grahame's 'relentlessly nice' characterization. To satisfy him, 'characters in a play need to go on a journey', an interior journey, as he makes quite clear in his introduction by analysing the disturbance and growth that Rat, Mole and Badger experience. One could read the play as a study of friendship, and of tension occurring when a new person enters an existing relationship. Badger becomes a nice old bachelor with a soft spot for little boys. Rat is practical, bossy and unaware of how much feeling he represses (Bennett comments that 'Toad, ... though a fool in all sorts of ways, still knows more about the heart than Rat'), but we are aware from the start that Rat is reluctant to introduce Mole to Badger and, when they do meet, he feels unacknowledged jealousy. When Grahame's Mole and Rat are saved by Badger, what upsets Rat and divides him from Mole is the fact of being underground. Otherwise, Mole and Rat constantly act in unison: we are told, for example, that the 'two friends assented' and 'both animals nodded gravely' and that eventually they sleep in identical beds. In Bennett's version, in direct contrast, Badger concentrates entirely upon looking after Mole, and repeatedly applies to him the word 'little', which Bennett avoids in the opening scene. Rat is unconsciously and not surprisingly jealous, so that he blames Mole for what has happened and, when Badger fetches Mole's soup and not Rat's, he is distinctly tart: 'Shall I get my own?' Finally, Mole gets the best sleeping place and bedding. The scene ends with Rat, just before he leaves Badger's home, looking round 'a little sadly', now that his relationship with it has changed, and for once he, not Mole, says 'Sorry' as he recognizes that the power structure of their relationships has shifted.

More complicated feelings also make the ending more open and ambiguous. The kisses which the gaoler's daughter gives Toad, Rat and Mole (it isn't 'Badger's thing at all') are Bennett's invention. He briefly admits women and sexuality into the asexual lives of Grahame's characters, which, as he says in the introduction, opens up new areas of growth and change, but also allows the possibility that the group of friends might break up, possibly with resentment and jealousy. Bennett, so preoccupied with secret, repressed inner lives in *Talking Heads*, *The Madness of George III* and the three spy plays, is not content with the ending which Grahame writes for Toad. Rather than changing his ways, Bennett's Toad stays unreformed. His irrepressible bumptiousness is not destroyed; he has merely learned that by concealing it he gets even more attention. But, through Mole, Bennett doubts that this change is for the better: it makes things 'dull'. For both these reasons, the end of the play is more unsettling than that of the book.

Bennett's sense of the outside threat to the pleasurable and innocent River Bank is as different from Grahame's as the inner complications of the characters. As he rejected the 'divine discontent' of the opening, Bennett rejects the abstract Terrors of the Wild Wood for something more concrete and human. Mole is mobbed by the Wild Wooders, who bait him like racist yobs at 'any provincial bus station on a Saturday night':

STOAT STUART: Go back to where you belong . . .
WEASEL NORMAN: We don't like little brown animals . . .
WEASEL WILFRED: Moles are dirty . . .

They beat him up, and later Rat tells Mole that 'It's just their nature'. To Bennett, the ugly side of human nature is terror enough. When Portly goes missing and Mole says that he 'hasn't an enemy in the world', Rat lists real enemies of otters: 'Hunters, with their long poles and those shameful dogs. Anglers. Gamekeepers'. Mole's come-back, 'In our world, I mean, Ratty', admits that Grahame's pastoral world denies and excludes much. 'That dark place on the horizon' which Rat does not want to talk about is lightly but definitely brought into the play. Rat, walking back to the River Bank, is nervously aware of 'someone . . . in the shadows watching them' and, preparing to eat in Mole's cosy house, is on the alert and made nervous again by a small noise. Presumably the director, Nicholas Hytner, who asked Bennett to keep the weasels constantly present on the stage, did so in order to keep a shadow of danger hanging over the idyll. So the weasels are on sentry duty outside Badger's safe house, a contrast to its cosiness and the obscure jealousies and attractions going on inside.

There is enough threat to pastoral here to have disturbed some adults in the audience. However, Bennett believes that children are matter-of-fact enough not to be disturbed by the baby rabbit being killed as prey or Mole's sister being killed to make a waistcoat. (After all, the adults' own generations were brought up on Peter Rabbit's father having been made into a pie.) Further, he uses comedy to defuse anxiety. The stage directions are flippant: the weasels 'snaffle from under the nose of its dozy mother a particularly succulent baby rabbit'; there are jokes: a 'fox with a conscience' explains about a hen who 'lost her head completely'. The weasels are allowed the comic heartlessness of Damon Runyon's gangsters:

WEASEL NORMAN: Of course, Chief, if I'd bitten their heads off when I wanted to we could have been fast asleep by now.
CHIEF WEASEL: Norman.
WEASEL NORMAN: Yes, Chief?
CHIEF WEASEL: Do you know what it's like to have your head bitten off?

As Bennett says in his introduction, the other major change he made was to turn the weasels who take over Toad's house into property developers and speculators. In his version of *The Wind in the Willows*, they represent the climactic threat to the two pastoral myths of England which the play dramatizes: the great house and the innocent River Bank home. Bennett has also added another figure who might be seen as embodying a similar threat, the motor car salesman. He says, 'Motor cars is progress, sir. Motor cars is the future', and sounds like a parody of E. M. Forster, who in *Howards End* associates the motor car with the commercial ethos which threatens his pastoral vision of England. Grahame's weasels are 'bloodthirsty villains', 'armed to the teeth' and violently beating up Mole and Badger. In addition to their armed violence, they do not work and are 'cocky', disorderly and vulgar. For these reasons, they used to be interpreted as a militant proletariat, as Bennett points out, but he seems to think that a militant proletariat can no longer be seen as a threat to the English pastoral. Instead, he uses the play to suggest that after Mrs Thatcher's decade the threat comes from capitalist materialism. In the play, the armed violence is lessened – as Toad does not go to Toad Hall to be shot at – and is sent up by parody when Bennett suggests 'a snatch of "The Dam Busters"'. Badger warns Toad that the house is 'a fortress'. This may be a military term, but is also used of the highly protected properties of the rich. The weasels, earlier identified as gangsters, begin to talk the language of board rooms ('I now call upon our beloved chairman'), and advertising ('a typical English country estate, run on traditional lines . . . comfortable . . . hospitable'). They betray the cynicism of the image maker ('shove on a marina, and a café or two to fetch in the tourists') and use dishonest euphemisms ('Three months of what you might call calculated decrepitude'). Again, Bennett makes them less frightening by turning them into a joke, this time by his satirical ear for modes of language.

The changes which Bennett made to Grahame's book are primarily aesthetic. He makes clear in the introduction to the text of the play that he found aspects of Grahame's characterization and 'lyrical' writing uncomfortably sentimental. He simply could not be satisfied with a play which retained these qualities, and he altered the characterization and tone accordingly. By doing this, he assimilated the book to his own particular dramatic strengths: a subtle account of psychological states and changing relationships, seen with an eye for both the absurdity and attraction of nostalgia. It is this that makes the play interesting for adults as well as children. That the weasels suggest some events of the 1980s is a minor part of the play, but it is interesting that, when his comic imagination sought for an up-to-date version of a group who threaten his ordinary characters as they get on with their lives, property developers are what occurred to him. The weasels, though they may be comic caricatures, imply Bennett's political sympathies.

The weasels reappear as Swaby and his group of friends in *A Private Function* and, in this darker and more satirical film, no heroic warriors arrive to break up the banquet in which they celebrate their power. The gentle English pastoral comedy of *Forty Years On* and *The Wind in the Willows* is darkened in *A Private Function* because, like *Enjoy*, it admits a much nastier human nature. The basic innocence which pastoral assumes disappears and the corrupt alternative against which it is so often implicitly set is moved centre-stage.

A Private Function

Bennett's fullest treatment of England as a consumer capitalist country is to be found in *A Private Function*. This is a film which was made in 1984 at the height of Mrs Thatcher's success. The film has a great deal of subject matter in common with the 1949 Ealing comedy, *Passport to Pimlico*, and comparing the two films is a useful way of seeing how radical his attack is on self-flattering myths of England and Englishness. The differences in handling the material are striking, and the result is that Bennett's 1984 picture of England is totally unlike Balcon's in 1949, and much less consoling. It can even be seen as a critique of some of the very myths about England which Balcon's assumes and supports.

A Private Function is set in Leeds in 1947, a time when food rationing was very severe and the wedding of Princess Elizabeth to Prince Philip was imminent. Led by Dr Swaby, several of the city's notables, who experience little difficulty in getting an adequate supply of meat for themselves, are bribing a farmer to raise an illegal pig to celebrate the royal wedding with a grand banquet. Joyce Chilvers, who lives with her chiropodist husband, Gilbert, and her ageing mother, has social aspirations and longs to be invited; Gilbert has plans to start up a chiropody surgery in the Parade, but is prevented from doing so by Swaby. The butchers in the town are 'on the twist' because of the meat shortage: Wormold, from the Ministry of Food, is trying to track down offenders. Nuttall, one of the butchers, uses his mistress, Mrs Forbes, in whose house Wormold lodges, to feed the Ministry man information about other butchers, forcing his competitors out of business.

Gilbert eventually discovers the hidden pig and, driven by hunger, humiliation, an angry sense of injustice and nagging by Joyce, steals it.

However, he cannot bring himself to kill it, even though it causes havoc in their house. Swaby discovers where it is and the group arrives to claim it back. To Gilbert's distress, Nuttall kills the pig on the premises. But Joyce now has knowledge which allows her to blackmail Swaby into inviting her family to the banquet. As the film ends, we see the celebration, the pig's head being paraded in, and Joyce promising Gilbert that in ten years' time they too will be at the top table.

Passport to Pimlico was made at a time when the sense of national unity and hope that had brought a Labour government to power after the war was fading. Europe was recovering faster than Britain, where there was still rationing of food and petrol; building was severely controlled; there was monetary crisis and devaluation in 1947, in whose long, hot summer Balcon's film appears to be set. (I say 'Balcon's film', in spite of the way he encouraged teamwork and the exchange of ideas in the Ealing studios. The small scale of the organization and the way he ran it seem to have allowed him to put a personal stamp on their productions. Certainly, in *A Biographical Dictionary of Film*, David Thomson speaks of Balcon rather than the studio as 'endors[ing] a conservative but independent England'.) Balcon, according to George Perry in *Forever Ealing*, was a 'moderate supporter of the Labour government' and to the young Perry in 1949 the film had seemed like 'an astonishing lampoon of the government and the mandarins of Whitehall'. But seen through modern-day eyes, it offers a comic daydream of escape from the discomforts of rationing and official control, affirming the admirable national qualities which won the war. Far from seeing the need for political change, it is fundamentally conservative and endorses entrenched class and power structures. Bennett's film, on the other hand, does not offer a daydream or assent to the status quo. On the contrary, it is critical about status, privilege, class antagonism and power structures created by money,

A Private Function was issued in 1984, near the beginning of the period which Kenneth Morgan in *The People's Peace* characterized as 'High Noon for the New Right' – 1983–9. Morgan, in this history of post-war England, sees those years as a period lacking in 'social compassion', and one in which the gulf between rich and poor became wider than at any period since the Second World War. He thinks that the prosperity of the rich came to depend on 'consumer pump-priming' rather than on mass manufacturing, and that during the miners' strike, Britain came near to 'open class war'.

Bennett's historian's accuracy leads him to note that the royal wedding took place in November, not, as the film has it, in the summer. He also uses his own memories – in 1947, his father was a butcher in Leeds and, even as a child, he knew that there were butchers 'on the twist'. Bennett's film is built on a knowledge of how things were.

A Private Function and *Passport to Pimlico* have much in common. The first is specifically set in the summer of 1947; the second is apparently so. Both stories centre on severe rationing and the possibility of avoiding it; both end with a celebratory banquet. There are also many smaller resemblances: both make use of the claim that the war unified the nation; both deal with two main social groups (petit bourgeois tradesmen and the middle class); both contain an episode which parodies a thriller. *Passport to Pimlico* even features a pig, which is briefly glimpsed dangling in a sling from a helicopter, during the air lift of food to the besieged 'Burgundian' citizens, and which is also presumably due to become bacon. Finally, both films begin by drawing attention to the differences between England and abroad.

Passport to Pimlico opens with a sequence which suggests that we are somewhere in southern Europe. There are shots of sun, sunblinds, a girl sunbathing, an outdoor café with parasols and a horse wearing a straw hat, while Latin-American music plays. Are we in the south of France or Spain? Then we find we have been misled. The camera slides down a shop awning to find a notice 'Frying Today' and we know we are in England. This is confirmed when the local policeman appears and we hear a radio announcer saying that the music was played by Les Norman and his Bethnal Green Bambinos. The joke is that somewhere so familiar should be mistaken for the exotic. Later, the joke will be that this ordinary piece of London *is* abroad: 'Blimey, I'm a foreigner!' is one of the famous lines. In other words, the comedy depends on the viewer assuming that England is *not* like abroad.

A Private Function opens with an old Pathé newsreel. The second item in this announces a cut in the bacon ration, and the commentator explains that in France rationing has caused a black market. The implication is that abroad is corrupt and money rules, whereas in England there are fair shares for all. The differences between England and abroad, however, are not suggested by images which the audience can see, as they are in *Passport to Pimlico*. They are stated by the anonymous voice of the news-reader in this, the official version of England. This time, the comedy comes from the discrepancy between actuality and England's official picture of itself, a picture which is present but not satirized in *Passport to Pimlico*.

In *A Private Function*, the embodiment of the official picture of England is the royal family. The first item in the opening newsreel is the

Royal Wedding, which is kept before us all through the film. The royal couple are constantly present: there are posters on the wall behind a queue in the butcher's, as well as in the hotel kitchen, as Dr Swaby's group snarl at each other about their dilemma; we hear background radio commentaries about them and they are repeatedly referred to as 'pure', 'noble' and 'unspoiled'. The respect shown to them is pushed to absurdity: Mrs Allardyce will not allow her toe-nail clippings to fall on a newspaper photograph of the Princess; someone is excluded from the banquet in the Royals' honour because his daughter was a pregnant GI bride. To the characters in the film the royal couple represent an idealized England, in contrast to the corruptions of abroad; for the audience, what they represent contrasts ironically with the corruptions of home.

The gap between England and abroad is further narrowed by implied parallels and resemblances. The film shows the English being just as corrupt as they claim the French are, giving similar priority to money, with the added implication that they are hypocritical or self-deceiving. The French may eat horsemeat – but a Leeds butcher is selling it too. The starving ate rats in Stalingrad, but Bennett's well-fed characters fight to eat a pig which was nourished on rats. Abroad, under the Gestapo, there was the sort of society where treachery and informers flourished. Wormold is compared to the Gestapo and is introduced sitting in the dark at the wheel of a car, observing a suspect's house, with a 'black-gloved hand drumming impatiently on [the] steering wheel'. Mrs Forbes is a treacherous informer: she tells Wormold about the butchers who sell illegal meat, and her betrayals lead to their arrests. When she passes Wormold the horsemeat she has just bought as proof of such an offence, she acknowledges the parallel when she says: 'They shaved women's heads for this in France.'

The central situation of *Passport to Pimlico* has analogies to Britain's situation during the war. Little Burgundy under siege by the Establishment uses many visual echoes to suggest England standing alone during its finest hour. There are familiar images of bombed landscapes, frontier posts, barbed wire, refugees with suitcases, children being evacuated, and the band of heroes in the dark on their dangerous mission. The qualities which the 'Burgundians' show, the film suggests, were those which won the war. What the film stresses is that they are a community: they all know each other and each other's children; policing can be done paternally; visually they move as a body when the initial explosion happens. The English in the film are generous to each other: rationing is forgotten as the film shows food being thrown and airlifted into

'Burgundy' with carnival extravagance. At the end, their return to England is celebrated as a community.

The myth of community which Balcon assumed also appears in *A Private Function*. Once again it is verbalized by the Establishment voice of news commentators speaking to and for the nation: 'The humanity which unites us all', announces one; according to the opening newsreel and later Wormold, the war was fought to ensure 'fair shares for all'. Admittedly, there is one moment in the film when Bennett's characters behave as Balcon's do: when the constable carries off a confiscated side of pork, which the Metcalfs are going to be punished for possessing, Mrs Metcalf puts a cloth between the meat and the constable's uniform because, 'Your mam'll play pop'. Here she speaks as one of a community where everyone is on kindly and personal terms with everyone else's family. Otherwise, every man is for himself in a society where wealth, represented mainly by food, is in short supply. Instead of community, there are corrupt alliances: between the policeman and the butcher; Mrs Forbes and Nuttall; Swaby and Sutcliff, the farmer. It is a mob, not a community, that threatens mass action outside the closed butcher's shop. Dr Swaby ('I don't know what the last war was about') betrays the fact that he sees the war as having been fought to keep him at the top of the heap. The whole film is a denial of the myth of 'fair shares for all': Mrs Allardyce has nylons and chocolates, and the film cuts tellingly from the Chilvers' sparse supper of tomato and spam to the Allardyces dining on steak and sprouts.

Balcon's England is sexually modest: Shirley is rebuked for answering the door in her (quite decent) sunsuit. Huggins sighs for the unattainable and settles for the nice, available girl. The only romance is of a mild and conventional kind between the Duke and Shirley, and even that is comically interrupted by a cat and a man gargling.

The 'purity' attributed to the lovers in *Passport to Pimlico* and to the royal couple in *A Private Function* contrasts sharply with the actual sexuality which Bennett shows in his film. Here, the only tender emotional attachment is to a pig, while the royal romance is constantly undercut. Mrs Forbes reads aloud about the royal wedding cake as Nuttall fancies having her 'bum' on his bacon-slicer, and she tells him to 'get on with it', which he does while she continues indifferently to read the paper. When Joyce announces that 'sexual intercourse is in order', or gets out an immense antique douche, Gilbert looks understandably apprehensive. Mrs Allardyce thinks that her husband is a pig. Dr Swaby's hand wanders lecherously to Joyce's bottom during the final dance. There is a gesture towards the conventional comic resolution of marriage when Wormold proposes to Mrs Forbes, but he seems to have no capacity for sensuous pleasure at all, his taste and smell having been destroyed by German measles.

The pastoral myth of England is only briefly present in *Passport to Pimlico*: the Minister's home in a pretty rural landscape. However, it is metaphorically there, since 'Burgundy' is an Eden. When the 'Burgundians' find that they are outside English law, somebody worries, 'Nobody cares if we get our throats cut', but actually there is nobody in the 'Burgundian' community capable of doing such harm. It is a stable and safe community, for all the residents' apparently revolutionary actions, and any threat is from without, from the government and the street traders, who are eventually expelled from this ration-free Paradise.

Bennett's initial outdoor shot is pastoral too: we see Gilbert and his bicycle in the beautiful Yorkshire dales. Later, pastoral reappears as Sutcliff's farm, which is squalid, and in which the pastoral flock is represented by Betty, the pig, which is fed an appalling diet, stinks (there is much play with handkerchiefs) and has diarrhoea. The English love of animals survives in the engaging but ineffectual Gilbert and the stupid Allardyce – theirs is the one friendship which crosses the class divide. Bennett's second assent to pastoral is that he makes the pig so appealing that we are on its side. No other character shares the pair's feeling: Nuttall is callously matter-of-fact about killing Betty, and the appalling Preston Sutcliff (a child, into the bargain) is itching to do it himself and sets off to visit the pig with a knife.

Balcon shows an England stratified by class between the petit bourgeois and the Establishment, who are shown exercising many public functions: Home Office, Foreign Office, Customs and Excise, Courts and the law, Bank officials, the local council – all are represented. There is a certain amount of crossover, since the bank manager and the eccentric professor both join the 'Burgundians'. The Establishment characters are just doing their job and are made neither corrupt nor vicious, since they will not let the 'Burgundians' starve to death. Petit bourgeois England is small-scale, community-minded, independent, generous, parochial, good-natured, and well able to negotiate with Whitehall. Though circumstances cause antagonisms between these two separate social groups, there is relief on both sides when a way back to unity is discovered.

This is particularly clear from the street party, which is the climax of the film. After all, what are they celebrating? They are returning to England, which means returning to ration books (a new ration book lies at every place), and to English rain and cold, for, as they start their banquet, the unnaturally hot weather of the rest of the film breaks and the rain descends. The joke seems to be that they like the discomforts of being English. More puzzlingly, they seem to be celebrating the loss of the way of life and the independence which they fought for during the film. They may have asserted their independence, but in the end they desire to be back inside hierarchical English society. The film seems to celebrate the qualities of petit bourgeois people who can resist political or administrative power, but do not want it for themselves. The film allows them an escape to a continental paradise, a moment of carnival freedom, but does not allow them power or political autonomy, for their state is based on improvised generosity, which will not sustain a social order by itself. They eventually find it desirable to return to the old order and, in this old order, power is in Establishment hands. The film suggests that both groups, amicably accepting this power structure, together make up 'England'.

A Private Function also sees England as a society split between petit bourgeois and Establishment. There has been no change in that between the film made in 1949 and the one in 1984. Gilbert is the same mild, good-natured type as Balcon's Burgundians, but Bennett is much more ambivalent about his virtues. There is a shocking and funny moment when Swaby's car carelessly knocks Gilbert off his bicycle. It is Swaby who is angry; Gilbert who smiles and apologizes. This is funny because it is so crazy, but shocking because Gilbert so automatically accepts his position in an unjust relationship. He blinds himself and is therefore not blameless. As in *Passport to Pimlico*, none of the characters wants to change the power structure, though here the audience is challenged by its implications. The discontented Joyce does not desire change, but instead to join the privileged: her talk is of rising 'to the top', 'status', 'get[ting] on'.

Balcon's Establishment comes into conflict with the 'Burgundians' as they administer the rules, but they are well-meaning, and have no personal animus or axe to grind. Nobody among them shows anything like Dr Swaby's vicious contempt and rage ('scum'; 'festering, bunion-scraping little pillock'), the ugly face of the stratified system. His anger seems to be largely a response to his fear that the power structure may be changing, when, in his view, the war should have preserved it. He would have the Socialists 'bastinadoed' and 'flayed alive'. To him, the NHS is a threat because it means that 'any little poorly pillock is henceforth going to be able to knock on my door and say, "I'm ill. Treat me." Anybody! Me!' He assumes the right to be moral spokesman and judge because, to him, morals are just another class privilege ('No class. No breeding. No morals.'). Yet he is arrogant: his car owns the road and Gilbert should not be in his way. He is petty, using his responsibility for planning permission to destroy Gilbert's hopes of a surgery. Also, in him we can see the English myth being used to retain Establishment power. He is the one who harps on the royal couple's purity, and he uses their wedding as an excuse to save his own face when he tells Gilbert that he is not going to report his theft to the police.

In both films, the class divide shows in voices. In *Passport to Pimlico*, the split is fairly simple. To have Received Pronunciation is to be marked as a 'responsible man', as the policeman says to Wix. There is an interesting exception: Shirley, who belongs to the petit bourgeois, uses Received Pronunciation and her parents do not. Presumably, without it she would not be a fit match for the Duke! But *A Private Function* has a voice which is missing from the earlier film: Maggie Smith's marvellous rendering of a just not quite right voice and idiom, would-be genteel, the voice of one aspiring to leave her class and always marked as not belonging to the other.

So Bennett's classes, unlike Balcon's, are not in a harmonious relationship. There is contempt on one side and discontent on the other. Bennett's characters are split between those who are included and those who are excluded, those who have and those who have not. When Gilbert is given his first piece of illegal meat, his response to Joyce is 'We're in'. Twice there is an image of a crowd staring into a closed butcher's shop through a glass door (a barrier through which they can see what they are being excluded from). To be an insider is to be one of the haves, especially having access to food, a scarce commodity which represents privilege, wealth and power.

Passport to Pimlico may be set during a time of strict rationing, but it is part of its comic fantasy that food is tossed with celebratory extravagance over the barricades and dropped randomly in huge quantities from helicopters. Generosity is shown in abundance. But in *A Private Function* food really is scarce, and it becomes an obsession. At the start, Joyce's mother is surreptitiously eating a sandwich, which she hides from the postman; Gilbert is then shown opening his lunch box and finding an old dishcloth inside, instead of his sandwich. Food is desired so much that shortage has led to stealing from one's family. There is as much emphasis on the royal wedding cake as there is on the royal couple: they are privileged to have the ingredients supplied from Australia. Most of Bennett's characters are hungry for power as well as food, and the film constantly links possession of food with status and power: 'It's not just steak, Gilbert . . . It's status', says Joyce, which she repeats as 'It's not just pork. It's power'. Possession of food is also linked to class. The Allardyces have steak, the Chilvers, spam; the butcher gives the police constable one chop and the inspector three. Joyce empties a precious tin of peaches into the scraps for the pig to show that she is also a 'have' and therefore an insider with a claim to power and status. Gilbert explains his theft as 'We were hungry', but what drives him to it is Joyce's rage and his own humiliation after Swaby has exercised his power, deprived him of his surgery and destroyed his bicycle. It makes them ready to steal, and even kill. There is clearly a parody of *Macbeth*, as Joyce urges the reluctant Gilbert to kill Betty: murder lurks in the background. When Swaby accepts Joyce's sweet sherry at the end of the film, it is a sign that power has passed into her hands. Food, like power, is often corrupted: the pig is raised on a terrible diet, including dead rats. A side of pork is painted green to make it unfit for human consumption and then scrubbed with bleach and served to customers – among them Wormold, who painted it green in the first place.

Common ground between the classes appears mainly in corruption and self-seeking. Dr Swaby is an accomplice of Sutcliff and Nuttall; the police inspector and butcher are in collusion. The plebeian Nuttall organizes a system of betrayal to the Gestapo-like authorities, and the other butchers are on the twist in more minor ways. More common ground is the alliance between Gilbert and Allardyce, who are brought together by their affection for Betty. They both take the class structure for granted, without aspiration to move out of it from Gilbert, and without contempt from Allardyce. The film ends with them cuddling their new piglet together. But even this image of harmony is qualified: both are despised by their own class and their alliance is only one between eccentric outsiders.

Both films end with a celebration dinner, but where the dinner in *Passport to Pimlico* celebrates a return to unity, the dinner in *A Private Function* celebrates something very different. In the royal wedding, they celebrate a myth in which there is no reality, but which is used to maintain the status quo. The dinner reaffirms the structure of the included and the excluded. There is a long debate about who should be invited and who should not, and clear anti-Semitism is shown when one possible guest is excluded. Joyce's triumph is just to be there, even if it is only near the Gents, inside not outside. She has joined the haves, though everything in the film suggests they are not worth joining. In sharp contrast to Balcon's street party, which dramatized contented acceptance of traditional power structures, Bennett's dinner dramatizes a much darker version of how these structures work. Morgan's description of England in the mid-1980s fits Bennett's England very well: it lacks compassion and justice, is primarily concerned with money and what it can buy, there is an enormous gap between rich and poor, and there is a vicious battle going on between them.

Much of the comedy in *Passport to Pimlico* comes from the incongruity of these stereotypically English people being foreigners, and the stereotypically English environment being a foreign country, as when London buses are going to England. It is a similar joke when Pemberton is called the Prime Minister, Wix, Chancellor of the Exchequer, and Molly, Minister for Supplies. In the teeth of the contemporary Labour government and Nye Bevan's building the National Health Service, the joke depends on our assumption that it is absurd that these people could ever hold such a post; that in real life, political power would never be in the hands of the petit bourgeois. It is like a Twelfth Night celebration, when inversion of social role and power is briefly allowed. The very basis of the comedy is a conservative assumption.

The comedy of *A Private Function* is based on a different sort of absurdity: the recurring contrast between the myth and the actuality of England. The comic climax is a long sequence of intercutting between the two, as the film shifts between the royal wedding and the pig being killed. As Nuttall goes off in Joyce's apron to kill Betty, he suggests that they need some noise to conceal the slaughter from Wormold outside. Joyce moves to the piano and plays Ivor Novello's 'Rose of England'. Bennett then cuts to Preston arriving to help Nuttall. Meanwhile, Joyce gossips admiringly about Princess Elizabeth, talks about the war, quotes Milton, and ends with: '. . . it's what we do best, isn't it, the pageantry? The carriages passing through the streets, the Household Cavalry, the bells ringing out. Oh, England. It's like a fairy tale'. Her picture of the best of England is one of picturesque preserved rituals of the past, the kind that tourists like to see. She approves of it as a living fairy tale, but in a different sense, a fairy tale is exactly what her England is, while the microcosm of England in Bennett's film is this group of unpleasant people pursuing their own ends of money and status in a small suburban house. 'I know they're going to be very happy', sighs Joyce romantically as Betty screams shrilly in her death throes upstairs and Nuttall comes down the stairs with two buckets of her blood, wishing he had time to make black pudding.

All this makes Bennett's comedy much darker than Balcon's. Apart from Swaby's viciousness, if the audience are English animal lovers and find Allardyce and Gilbert the characters with whom they most easily identify, then the unfeeling slaughter of the animal at the end comes as a shock. In his introduction, Bennett wrote that he had not eaten pork since the film was made, and he adds that the final scene with the piglet was put in to soften the effect of Betty's death. Further, if one expects the conventions of comedy to be preserved in a comic film, then one probably expects Betty to be saved, especially as so much laughter is produced by the parody of *Macbeth* and the failure of Joyce and Gilbert's attempts to kill her. All this is a sharp contrast to the pig at the end of *Passport to Pimlico*, where it is merely a momentary and ludicrous image.

Another myth of England which the film challenges is one about the English sense of humour. *Passport to Pimlico* flatters us by asking us for laughter that is only gentle, self-mocking, causes no pain and delights in the absurd. There is nothing worse than our own absurdity to laugh at, and we can do that with unqualified enjoyment. Almost forty years later, at the height of Mrs Thatcher's competitive, money-driven economy, Bennett builds his comedy on a painful awareness of England's illusions about itself and what it actually is. And this demands of the English a different sense of humour: one which is much more uncomfortable and much more savage.

PART TWO

Speaking for the Unheard

4 The Lady in the Van

A major concern of Bennett's work is to speak for those whose voices are not normally heard in public, on television, the stage or in books. This has been a part of English literature since nineteenth-century novelists such as Dickens, George Eliot and Hardy, but emerged rather later in drama. Pre-war dramatists such as Lawrence, and Galsworthy in *Strife*, post-war dramatists such as Osborne, Wesker, Delaney and Pinter have all, in various ways, tried to create voices for the unheard.

Bennett's voices include most of the characters from his northern plays and the *Talking Heads* monologues, who are made socially and politically powerless by geography, class, education and gender or, like the Chinese waiter in *Afternoon Out*, by culture and language. Many are marginalized by age, like the couples in *Sunset Across the Bay* and *Enjoy*. There are also the upper-class spies, who for much of their lives could not speak the truth about themselves. They still resort to deflections like irony (Hilary), metaphor (Blunt) and jokes which tell truths that nobody will believe (Burgess). Through them, especially in *A Question of Attribution*, Bennett explores the unvoiced secret self, the privacy of the personality, which his Kafka also defends strenuously in *Kafka's Dick*. Through King George III, unable to let his secret self be heard except in madness, he voices the silenced areas of the personality which the process of socializing normally teaches us to conceal, and which he also gives voice to in Toad, as Ian Buruma in the *New York Review of Books* (February 1995) pointed out. The Talking Heads famously betray what their minds do not know and they cannot admit to themselves. Bennett gives a hearing to voices marginal to his own life through the unidentified voices transcribed into the diaries and orchestrated in *Dinner at Noon* and *Portrait or Bust*, the documentary programmes about a hotel and an art gallery. Miss Shepherd, the lady in the van, marginalized by homelessness and derangement, is not an odd woman out in Bennett's work, but one of a crowd.

Bennett himself is well aware of this preoccupation: as he concludes in *The Lady in the Van*: 'the location of most of the stuff I write about . . . is to the side and never what faces me'. The location of these voices may be to the side, but if they do not face Bennett, he faces them: he looks intently at what normally goes unnoticed. Miss Shepherd may be the focus of *The Lady in the Van*, but in the short piece Bennett attends to other unacknowledged lives as well: the 'small acts of heroism' of the doctor, the priest and the social worker who go into the awful van 'without distaste or ado', and also the ambulance man who arranges her clothes with the same lack of reaction.

Yet to write and to publish is to have a voice. It is a paradoxical task for a published writer to give the voiceless a say. Bennett has experimented with different formal means of doing this, as varied as *The Lady in the Van*, *Talking Heads*, *The Madness of George III*, and *Sunset Across the Bay*, and has thereby uncovered a remarkably wide range of personality and experience.

Someone once said to me, 'What Bennett says is not so unusual, but his voice is unique.' Though there should be a distinction between the heard voice of the writer and the voices he desires to make heard, his own style will inevitably take theirs over as he writes them. Bennett said that Miss Shepherd lived in a gap 'between our social position and our social obligations'; in the work she lives in other gaps: between fact and fiction; writer and subject; his voice and hers. Bennett manages to use the fact that her voice has to be mediated through his to make hers more convincing. Indeed, he may even have responded to hers imaginatively because they have some qualities in common.

Miss Shepherd was not a fictional character. She really lived, and Bennett is interested in communicating her otherness and reality. *The Lady in the Van* is the account of an eccentric and homeless woman who lived for years in a van parked in the front garden of Bennett's own house. It consists mainly of extracts from the diaries which he kept during those years. There is a photograph of her in *Writing Home*, but it communicates very little of her individuality and strangeness. For that, we need her actual words, which Bennett apparently transcribes and reports. The piece opens with her saying: 'I ran into a snake this afternoon . . . It was coming up Parkway. It was a long, grey snake – a boa constrictor possibly . . . It was keeping close to the wall and seemed to know its way. I have a feeling it may have been heading for the van.' We recognize at once that this voice is in some way deranged: to see a boa constrictor in a London street, even near Regents Park zoo, is odd enough. To say matter of factly that it is behaving like a cautious and purposeful human is odder still. The impression that she is out of touch with reality is reinforced when she discusses being nominated as a parliamentary candidate, or offers to help Mrs Thatcher with the economy, or fears that General Galtieri may have mistaken her sympathy with his action in the Falklands for Mrs Thatcher's.

She has a distinctive style of speech. She garbles idioms like 'pedalling water' and uses unusual combinations of adjective and noun, such as 'Mattering Things', 'my cooperative part' and 'gigantic ignorant conduct'. She has a characteristic vocal tic, the recurrent word 'possibly'. It helps to give her speech an idiom and rhythm which is recognizable in the letter addressed to 'Mr Bennett, if necessary', and indicates (possibly!) that she had some doubts about her own strange assertions. It is also an educated voice. She knows the derivation of 'statutory' and uses dated slang like 'my spree', though she fails to cope with the more modern 'freebie'. In her filthy and eccentric life, she preserves polite conventions – she and Bennett always call each other 'Miss Shepherd' and 'Mr Bennett' – and respectabilities: 'I don't think this style can have got to Tunbridge Wells yet', she says of her strange clothes; 'I haven't been able to do any spring cleaning', she says as, in dying, she leaves the hideous mess she has never attempted to clean up.

Her logic is equally strange, which makes many of her utterances crazy and comic. For example, she says of a toad, 'I think he may be in love with the slug. I tried to turn it out and it got very disturbed. I thought he was going to go for me.' She argues with Bennett about her wish for the same kind of wheelchair as the boy across the road: 'Me: Miss Shepherd, he has spina bifida. Miss S: Well, I was round-shouldered as a child.' Here and elsewhere, her logic passes into *non-sequiturs*, as when she says of failing to become a nun, 'If I could have had more modern clothes, longer sleep and better air, possibly, I would have made it.'

Her derangement is reinforced by what is reported of her appearance and of her strange clothes, which are as garbled and incongruous as her speech and logic. Bennett also catches a characteristic pose: 'not looking un-crucified herself'. Above all, he catches her fierce secrecy and her pain. She, like so many of Bennett's fictional characters, is tragi-comic. He reports that there are 'few occasions on which one saw Miss Shepherd genuinely happy' and that he rarely sees her smile. When he registers that her face lights up with pleasure when she allows herself to freewheel in her wheelchair, her pleasure in this minimal satisfaction has a sad side.

So she is given to us apparently unmediated. Her clothes are listed, her facial expressions reported, her utterances and her letters transcribed and reproduced. Did Bennett transcribe them in his diary during all those years? That is what we are led to assume. His piece is an example of a particular kind of writerly virtue: scrupulous, accurate attention to what is the case. He sets out to reproduce her voice with both the comic writer's detached relish of the odd, and the compassionate writer's belief that if we hear it she will have a 'place in people's affections'.

But she is not unmediated, of course. Even if Bennett has transcribed her words accurately, he has selected what to include and he has embedded it in his own speech. Because his voice is one we can trust, we accept his account of her and believe we hear her clearly. What is remarkable about Bennett's account of his dealings with Miss Shepherd is how normal his feelings are. That he reveals their normality is surprising in itself. It is very difficult to relate to the disadvantaged without rejection, guilt or pity, which distort perception, and to tread the borderlines between patronage and compassion, or sympathy and laughter. He seems to react to her as just another human being, and is scrupulous about reporting what these reactions are. They are 'mixed' and often 'enraged'. He feels 'distaste' at her filthy van and when she wants to use his lavatory, 'on the threshold of the toilet ... my charity stopped short'. He is 'ashamed' to be seen mending her car. He is exasperated by her: 'One seldom was able to do her a good turn without some thoughts of strangulation.' He argues with her instead of humouring her, and he makes jokes about her, fully aware of her as comic, which is a further refusal to patronize the disadvantaged. 'Sense is needed,' announces Miss Shepherd. 'Hygiene was needed too,' comments Bennett. He wonders whether the bath she had just before she died had killed her. He sees himself as comic too, when he fantasizes about visiting her conventionally in hospital or when he is manipulated into pushing her to the launderette, and surprisingly does not feel guilty about his reluctance, as 'she knows exactly what she's about'. He notices the tragi-comic incongruity of 'Hands in mittens made from old socks, a sanitary towel drying over the ring, and a glossy leaflet from the Halifax offering "fabulous investment opportunities"' and also the 'chaos' of her life and the way she 'trips with fanatical precision' through the 'minefield' of Catholic liturgy. One may have wondered whether Bennett's own voice, self-deprecating, ironic, joking, compassionate, was another dramatic creation of a persona: here one has one's answer. Miss Shepherd guarantees his truth as he guarantees hers.

Bennett further voices the unheard in the way in which he handles what is usually taboo, and in doing so he confirms Miss Shepherd's separateness. During the first manned space flight, we wondered how the astronauts washed and excreted, and that curiosity about these basic needs was never satisfied because they were never talked about. Bennett, whose northern characters constantly talk about lavatories, keeps before us the practical problems of living without one and without a bathroom. Miss Shepherd smelled: 'She wants me to put a notice on the gate to the effect that the smell is the manure, not her. I say no, without adding, as I could, that the manure actually smells much nicer.' When he raises the question of her 'toilet arrangements' he writes of what he has seen: the plastic bags which she throws out of the van, the used sanitary towels, the 'stained incontinence pad', the shit-stained feet. It is a further confirmation of her reality and otherness that he says nothing else because he does not know exactly what is happening: she is 'now, I think, more or less incontinent'. If this were a work of fiction, he could invent any reality he chose, knowing the answers. As it is, we remain unsure when her incontinence starts; the sanitary towels and the incontinence pads appear without explanation, presumably supplied by somebody else, and what those black bags contain never transpires. The writer can give us no privileged access to another person's mystery, but he can and does pay attention.

At times the gap between their voices closes, or at least one can be seen as a version of the other. This is comic and surprising because the gap between them is in other ways so immense and one which Bennett resists closing: he is 'shocked at this tentative bracketing of our conditions' when she speaks of 'celibates like you and me' and he rejects the identification by getting rid of her. But common ground is undeniable and perhaps it enabled him to identify with her when he was creating her voice. After her death, he searches her van, and is disconcerted to discover that her way of life was in some ways like that of ordinary people: she had 'appurtenance[s] of gentility', like a condiment set stored but not used, just as his mother had, and he recognizes 'proprieties and aspirations no different from those with which I had been brought up'.

Moreover, she is just the kind of character that Bennett is strongest at: tragi-comic as well as marginalized. Quite literally, she offers herself as his subject: she suggests that a cameraman following her in a car might well get comic footage. As she says acutely, 'Comedy happens without trying sometimes.' Certainly much of Bennett's comedy arises out of accurate observation of the ordinary world. This is precisely what Miss Shepherd voices when she says, 'That would make a comedy, you know – sitting on a bus and your bus-pass out of date.' She seems to share Bennett's way of linking comedy and tragedy ('I was a born tragedian', she says, 'or a comedian possibly'), and comedy and pain ('People trip over me. That's comedy. I wish they didn't, of course').

She lives in another gap as well, between her fierce secrecy about herself and her desire to speak to the world. Bennett emphasizes her unwillingness to let herself be known. He knows very little about her history until after her death. It is touching when she trusts him enough to tell him tiny scraps of it: she has chauffeured renovated army vehicles and tried to become a nun but failed. However, she will not generally enter into conversations. If anyone speaks to her she will 'wordlessly' shut the door and 'wait, like an animal that has been disturbed'; she shuts the window on him when he asks her 'Why?'; she urges 'Don't tell anybody', 'Don't mention it to anybody'. Her final message, left to be opened after her death, gave away no more than a man's name and phone number. It is appropriate that she is finally laid in an unmarked grave.

Yet the paradox is that Miss Shepherd is a writer and sells pamphlets, though she will not admit that she wrote them. As she says in her characteristically garbled idiom – she too is an author with a unique voice – 'so far as the authorship is concerned I'll say they are anonymous and that's as far as I'm prepared to go'. She writes letters to Enoch Powell, Mrs Thatcher, the President of Argentina and the College of Cardinals, because she feels she has advice to give, something to say. She is willing to be nothing more than a voice: she would like to have a radio programme or to be on television provided she could be hidden behind a curtain, but she wants her voice to be broadcast, and suggests that a film or a comedy could be made about her.

This dual desire, to be heard and to protect the secret self, is a paradox which Bennett identifies as the writer's in *Kafka's Dick*, *A Question of Attribution* and in Burgess's line, 'No point in having a secret if you make a secret of it.' Presumably, it is something Bennett identified with in Miss Shepherd. When she dies, he regrets his own voicelessness and wishes to broadcast what he has to say: 'I regret too all the questions I never asked her . . . I have a strong impulse to stand at the gate and tell anyone who passes.' Eventually, the impulse won: the work itself, now widely read and known, tells more people than a few passers by. He has broadcast her voice for her – literally in radio talks and in print that has found wider circulation than her pamphlets ever did. But of course he has ignored her 'Don't tell anybody'. The paradox of the arts identified by Auden in *The Sea and the Mirror* is true: they cannot give voice to the one who refuses to be assimilated. Bennett creates her voice from the gap between the secret self and the desire to speak. In creating the secrecy he violates it; in creating the voice, he grants her wish. One wonders what she would have made of her fame. Has he broken faith? It is not a question one needs to ask about a fictional character. That he makes us ask it is further confirmation that Bennett has spoken for a very real and truly unheard person.

Bennett's work shows him to be interested in the borderline between fact and fiction and in finding forms to negotiate this borderline. One thinks of his two 'spy' plays, especially *An Englishman Abroad*, an artful piece of imaginative writing in which Coral Browne had what must have been the extraordinary experience of playing herself as a partly fictional character; the television programmes about the hotel and the art gallery; and *The Lady in the Van*. It is difficult to know what to call the work – prose fiction, diary, memoir, biography, auto-biography – which only indicates the subtlety of Bennett's solution to the formal problem. He had a choice when he opted for the diaries which allow interplay between their two voices. There is a possible fictional form which he rejected, even though he did use some devices from prose fiction to shape his work.

Miss Shepherd is a loner, an unheard, marginalized and tragi-comic voice, like the characters in *Talking Heads*. But if Bennett had written her as a monologue he could not have produced the voice he did. She is more secret and enigmatic than any of the Talking Heads, and Bennett could not have created her characteristic taciturnity in a monologue. She says the minimum about herself to her most trusted audience – him – whereas the Talking Heads, trusting their audience completely, confide freely. We hear the secret voices of the Talking Heads. They obey the convention that in soliloquy the character speaks the truth as it appears to them. Further, the Talking Heads are explored and understood, even though they may not understand themselves as the audience and writer do.

With Miss Shepherd, however, Bennett recorded what he saw and heard and made some deductions, but he does not hear her secret voice and does not invent it. Miss Shepherd retains her secrecy in a way that none of the Talking Heads manage. Though some things about her personal history are explained at the end, like the car accident which made her hide from the police, several mysteries remain: her life in the convent and the army; her toilet arrangements, to name but two. For example, what did she use all that talc for? That Bennett does not turn her into a Talking Head is his guarantee that he has not invented her, and is not an omniscient author who can account for her or explain her. Of course, we do not know everything about the Talking Heads either, but we know that we understand all we need to. In a work of fiction, the information that the writer chooses to give us about a character is enough to 'foreground' the writer's concerns and enable us to infer what we need to know. In *The Lady in the Van*, the writer and the reader both have to make do with what is available. Bennett may have searched the van for information, but he did not have the control over what he found that fiction would automatically grant. There is no guarantee that the most significant things about her are available to him or us.

Writing speech for the deranged is a problem in drama and fiction. Lady Macbeth and Ophelia break down convincingly, but everything they say is the invention of a sane mind controlling a complex structure of which they are part. A less successful madwoman like the girl in *The Man of Feeling* visibly draws on the same dramatic conventions for representing madness: she is a reach-me-down Ophelia. It is difficult to represent the processes of a deranged mind, because all works of litera-ture are purposefully patterned, and the inventing minds of (most!) authors are sane. One wants to say that Miss Shepherd's praise of Bath ('That looked nice. Some beautifully parked cars') or her crazy logic about the toad in love with the slug are beyond invention, but they aren't. A comic genius like Bennett could easily have invented them. However, once again, by refusing to write her as a monologue, Bennett has formally guaranteed that Miss Shepherd's derangement is outside his control.

The work is on the edge of autobiography, shaped out of snippets from Bennett's diaries and built up as a patchwork of short anecdotes and odd facts. There is no sustained utterance as there is in a mono-logue. The diary entries are written in the present tense, but there are sections which shift into the past, a more usual tense for prose fiction. For example, the passage on her political views, the history of the vehicles she owned and a summary of events near the end of her life are all in the past tense. This enables Bennett to combine random, fleeting glimpses of Miss Shepherd in speech or action, and then, as an author, to gather the material together and reflect on it.

The extracts from the diary are not random. They have been shaped, sometimes in a similar way to how fiction is worked. The piece opens *in medias res* with Miss Shepherd's voice, catching the audience's atten-tion as she announces that she had seen a snake in Parkway. (I am reminded of the opening sentence of *The Towers of Trebizond*: ' "Take my camel, dear", said my Aunt Dot, as she climbed down from this animal on her return from High Mass'.) Context and information are not supplied until the second paragraph. Further, Bennett anticipates later events, thus predetermining plot: 'Miss S. applied the handbrake with such determination that . . . when the van came to be moved ten years later it had to be hoisted over the wall by the council crane.' We are prepared for her dying by hints of her deterioration: 'Her legs are so thin now that the feet are as slack and flat as those of a camel'; 'now, I think, more or less incontinent'. A large proportion of the work is given to the last months of her life, concentrating on the time of maximum interest. The climax given by her death is extraordinary, and Bennett confesses that in his first draft he had played it down in case readers felt he had twisted the story into something 'sentimental or melodramatic'. Miss Shepherd is formally, ritually prepared for death: she is taken to a day care centre, washed, given clean clothes and bedding, and returned to her van, where she dies. Bennett even supplies elegiac consolation: 'a bee buzzing round her body. It is a beautiful day, with the garden glittering in the sunshine, strong shadows by the nettles, and bluebells out under the wall.' He makes the concrete serve as metaphor: 'the van in front but to the side of where I write' suggests 'the location of most of the stuff I write about' and the 'oil patch that marked the site of the van has long since gone, and the flecks of yellow paint on the pavement have all but faded'. Finally, as some modern novelists do, Bennett supplies alternative endings, the first ironic and sad, the second, written after he had more information, reflecting on how her 'bold life' compared to his own, and the third about her unmarked grave. Out of these delicate balances, the unheard voice, comic and pathetic together, is brilliantly given utterance.

5   Talking Heads

'Not English I feel now. This is just where I happen to have been put down. No country. No party. No Church. No voice', Alan Bennett observed in his diary extracts in *Writing Home*, written as the Falklands war was ending. With his rejection of his country's involvement in the war came the feeling that he belonged to no English community. He was marginalized, isolated, and the result, curious in such a popular writer, is that he felt that he had no voice. As Tony Harrison's poems constantly point out, to be voiceless is to be powerless, both personally and politically, and to vanish from the stage of history.

Bennett's Talking Heads are also marginalized and have had no voice – not until Bennett gave them one and allowed them to talk to the mass audience which TV provides. The first of his dramatic monologues, not one of the *Talking Heads* series, was significantly called *A Woman of No Importance*. It is noticeable that there is only one monologue for a man; the other five (six, counting the earlier work) are all for women. Three of the characters are northern, four of them middle-aged or old. Only Lesley, of *Her Big Chance*, is young and without a specific social and geographical background, and in my opinion this is the least successful monologue. Until recently, much English drama has been about the middle classes and for male actors. Though this is now less true of theatre and even less true of television, Bennett's alternative voices are still rare, perhaps because of their age as well as their gender, region and class. Even the one male part – acted by Bennett himself – is a type of character that recurs in his plays. However, as he admits in the preface to *The Writer in Disguise*, the character is not much fun to write, since he is a social outsider for whom 'Grrr' or 'Oh dear' is usually sufficient dialogue.

In one way or another, Bennett draws attention to this lack of voice in all the monologues. Lesley is stupid enough to be sexually exploited without realizing it, and is convinced she is an actress, when she cannot act. Although the monologue is an attack on her self-deception and egotism, the reality which Bennett suggests through his irony is that she is marginal, both in the acting world and the films she appears in. She had a non-speaking appearance in Polanski's *Tess* and was an extra in a party scene in *Crossroads*, where her voice was just part of the background noise. Her 'big line' in her present film is the single word 'Alfredo'. Originally it was 'I can't help it, Alfredo, I have a headache', but the director decided to cut it. Because 'it's all [she's] got to build on', the name of her character matters to her so much that she christens her short appearance in *Tess* 'Chloe'.

Irene Ruddock, the lady of letters, is lonely and afraid to go out. The only form of communication she has with people is the letters that she writes to public figures and strangers in a world in which she is a peripheral and mistaken observer. Oddly and comically, it is not until she is sent to prison, among other outcast women, that she finds a community where she can belong. She learns a new voice there, even though it is coarse and awkward for her. ('Fuck up', she says, instead of 'Fuck off'.) Now, she uses her letter writing to help others, and uniquely among the Talking Heads, she is freed from her earlier entrapment to be happy.

Doris, in *A Cream Cracker Under the Settee*, is an elderly northern widow, whose one child was born dead. She laments the loss of a community in which 'folks smiled and passed the time of day'. Now, she is fighting to remain in her home, being bossed (albeit sensibly) by her home help, who lets her know that she is 'on trial' and being reported on. When the monologue starts, she has fallen and broken her hip. Doris knows that she needs to make her voice heard in order to get help, but she fails over and over again: a child pees at her gate, and she shouts him away; mail comes but the postman retreats. But at the end, when the policeman speaks to her through the letterbox, she sends him away, perhaps because she realizes that to be heard now would not be empowering but would lead to her final loss of autonomy.

Susan, the vicar's wife in *Bed Among the Lentils*, is a repressed and subversive voice. Bennett says that the idea for the piece came to him from finding the words 'Get lost, Jesus' written in 'tiny, timid letters' in a hymn book at his school. Susan has 'always longed to ask' her husband whether he believes in God, but 'the subject's never discussed'. On the ordination of women, '[she] wanted to say' that as far as she is concerned services can be taken by 'a trained gorilla' but she does not, and her husband answers for her: 'Susan's all in favour.' His voice swamps and is substituted for hers. Her moments of spoken resistance are modest, as when she deliberately misunderstands Geoffrey. When she does speak out and objects to Mrs Shrubsole's flower arrangement on the altar, she is drunk, so her voice can safely be ignored. When she wonders if Jesus had a sense of humour or was fully human, she is first patronized and then deserted. The only successful communication she relates is her cross-cultural adultery with the Hindu Mr Ramesh, which leads her to admit to her alcoholism. But even at Alcoholics Anonymous meetings '[she] never say[s] anything at all' about how she got to be there. The final bitter irony is that this silence keeps her permanently trapped in Geoffrey's version of events. His idiom, not hers, has the last word: 'We met it with love'; 'It's a great challenge to me and to the parish as extended family'.

The repressed Graham of *A Chip in the Sugar* is another isolate. He is middle-aged, still living with his mother, has a history of mental breakdown, delusions of being watched, and retreats to his bedroom when distressed. He substitutes pornographic magazines for relationships with people, has no job and the only community he belongs to is the 'Community Caring down at the Health Centre'. He is jealous of a man that his mother wants to marry, and eventually fights him off, though not overtly. The monologue is punctuated with 'I didn't say anything', which occurs five times, and with withdrawals like 'I went to the toilet' and 'I'm going to bed'.

Muriel's voice in *Soldiering On*, is the only non-marginalized voice in the series. Significantly, the voice is not northern, and belongs to the prosperous middle classes. Muriel lives in Suffolk, and uses a rather dated slang, which marks her age and social background: 'two brave souls'; 'we lived to fight another day'; 'absolutely chocker'; 'to blub'; 'hurling ourselves back into the fray'. Alone among the monologues, this voice is socially confident and competent, used to being in charge, used to dealing with tricky situations and people. 'I can talk to anybody', she says, and she does. The secretary of the hospital and the Hare Krishna devotee confide in her.

Though her voice does not change, we see it becoming marginalized in the course of the monologue. This is caused by many factors: her husband's death, her son's fraud, her consequent poverty, moving out of her home into temporary accommodation, and the loss of the community in which she functioned. She feels sure that 'there must be a community' in which she could be useful, and has 'a word' with a woman in the Town Hall, only to find that her skills are not wanted and that the person who was once '2 i/c Meals on Wheels for the whole of Sudbury' is now seen as a passive recipient of them. Poverty means that she can afford only an occasional 'natter' over coffee with a friend. By

the end of the monologue, she has become a passive watcher of '\
plugs her ears with a Walkman, keeping the world out. (Bennett \
diaries describes a mother using a Walkman and ignoring her cr\
baby.) Like Graham, she has retreated into silence.

It is to these marginalized, timid and hitherto bottled-up voices that
Bennett gives expression and the respect of attention. He allows us to
overhear them saying what remains unspoken in their fictional world, a
world whose presence and pressures on the characters are convincingly
included. Monologues by definition cannot use several defining features
of drama: the interaction of characters, dialogue, the meeting and clash-
ing of voices and points of view, the population of the world of the play
by other characters. However, Bennett manages to create a detailed
network of relationships for each Talking Head by means of reported
conversations with others. He also makes observations about their
appearance: Mr Turnbull, with his yellow gloves and little suede coat,
who thinks 'it's the blacks'; Mrs Shrubsole, who did the Forest
Murmurs plant arrangement for her 'Highly Commended at Harrogate
last year'; Angela Gillespie, who 'nipped in' to earmark Ralph's clothes
for Muscular Dystrophy. The isolation of Irene, in *A Lady of Letters*, is
implied by the way reported conversation is handled: the text contains
no reported conversation for the first four pages; then there are conversations reported with professionals – doctor, vicar, police and social
workers, of whom, for the first time, she uses a first name. Part of the
release of the final scene comes from the sudden flood of people with
whom she is on first name terms, and the amount of gossip and chat
that is reported.

Physical environments are created by casual references. Graham's
town has public lavatories, a war memorial that is also a roundabout, a
refined café and a common one, Tesco, Sainsbury's, BHS, and a community day care centre. In contrast, in *Her Big Chance*, we know nothing of Lesley's background, family or friends. The environments in
which she is photographed tell little; she says little about where she
lives; no secondary characters are vividly realized. The point may be
how rootless she is and how superficial her contacts are, but the
dramatic effect is that she floats in a vacuum, and the monologue feels
less substantial than the others in the *Talking Heads* series.

Creating a social and physical world by reporting in the past tense
what has been done, seen and said is a strategy primarily of narrative
fiction. Equivalents of *Talking Heads* in the genre of the novel are such
narrative monologues as *Catcher in the Rye* and *The Remains of the
Day*. However, where narrative fiction has listeners only by convention,

television drama has literally millions of them. Bennett's triumph is transferring their secret voices to the public medium of drama and using the strength of television as a medium.

In the monologues, the moments from which we make connections and read character are highlighted by their being shaped in a way peculiar to drama: by light and silence. They are beautifully constructed mini-plays, with the blackouts marking scenes and climaxes. In *A Chip in the Sugar*, for instance, the first scene is an exposition of the relationship between Graham and his mother and the meeting with Mr Turnbull. During it, there are two significant pauses, taken after ' "You'll make my boy friend jealous." I didn't say anything' and after 'I went to the toilet'. These highlight what Graham is not aware of: that he is 'married to his mother' and that he withdraws from confrontations and his own jealous feelings. The first blackout confirms this, after 'You're my boy friend, aren't you, Graham?'

In the second scene, Mother goes out with Mr Turnbull, leaving Graham. The blackout here comes when he fears his delusions are returning. This is the first we hear of his mental troubles. In the third, Mother is planning to marry, and it ends with Graham unable to sleep because a car is parked outside (a persecution fantasy?). At the end of the fourth scene, he sits fearfully in the dark. This time, however, the watcher turns out to be real, and is admitted. The fifth section sees Graham using this visit to defeat Mr Turnbull and reinstate himself, and the monologue ends with the status quo being restored, signalled by a dialogue which echoes the opening. The emphasis provided by the rhythm of blackout and pause brings us a deepening knowledge of Graham's mental abnormalities and growing anxieties, although Graham himself continues to deny them. Other threads which bind the monologue together are initiated and intensified: in the first scene, he buys 'some reading matter'; just before the blackout at the end of the second, he goes to bed with 'one of my magazines'. At the end of the fifth scene, Graham records his mother's implication that they are homosexual pornography. Then he pauses. Now we see him saying nothing and ignoring what has been said. When he speaks again, it is to say that his mother has 'forgotten it'. The status quo is restored and his denials continue. As in his therapy group, he cannot see that *he* is the problem.

Again, in *Bed Among the Lentils*, the rhythm created by the blackouts emphasizes significant moments. In the first scene, Susan's sexual dissatisfaction is established, and it ends with her going out to buy sherry. We are invited to notice this, though we do not understand its significance at this point. At the end of scene two, she meets Ramesh, who has a shop which sells 'drink and anything really', tho she says nothing about what she went there to buy. In the third sce_, she collapses after noticing flowers that 'could do with an immediate drink', and rummaging in the cupboard where Geoffrey keeps communion wine. Finally, she sleeps with Mr Ramesh.

Part four has Susan's first experience of sexual satisfaction, and this time ends with the overt indication of her alcoholism, 'He's put a lock on the cupboard door'. Scene five opens with her looking much smarter, and saying 'I am an alcoholic'. The denial has stopped and she is doing something positive, though the end comes with a return to her initial resentment towards her husband and God.

While the blackouts in *Bed Among the Lentils* invite us to notice what the character denies, those in *A Lady of Letters* encourage us to be deceived along with the character. Before each of the first four blackouts, Miss Ruddock describes her neighbours in ways which make us assume they are abusing their child. We learn the truth at the same time she does, at the fifth blackout.

The least satisfactory of the monologues, *Her Big Chance*, is the one in which the blackouts are the least informative. At the end of four out of the five scenes, Lesley goes to bed with a different man. That Bennett shapes the play by pausing for emphasis at so many similar points stresses the fact that Lesley sleeps around. But whereas Susan's sexual experience is central in her monologue and its meaning is clear to her, Lesley's is not. What Bennett emphasizes about her character is her self-deluding conviction that she is a serious actress and can build characters (even when she has virtually no material), not to mention her perky self-deception that she succeeds. We see and she ignores the fact that she is taking part only in a porn video, something which would upset her view of herself – though she betrays herself with her offer to simulate sexual intercourse at the climax of the video. The trouble with the piece is that there is no clear connection between what most interests Bennett in the character and the casual promiscuity, emphasized by the way he shapes the monologue.

Bennett uses the dramatic rhythm of scene and pause to emphasize and develop themes from episode to episode. These are themes which are important to the dramatist but which the character either denies or is unaware of. Much of the irony, pain and comedy of the monologues comes from this difference of perception.

If Bennett has abandoned the present tense of drama by choosing the past tense of the monologue, the character's 'now' is made clear by another means belonging only to visual drama: the language of set, lighting, costume, body language, facial expression and vocal inflections. Bennett uses the strengths of television: the small screen deals most effectively with the details of the expressive face in close-up. Television also allows the quiet, unemphatic voice to be heard; no theatrical projection is necessary.

Maggie Smith's body language at the opening of *Bed Among the Lentils* reveals her tension and lack of physical charm: the crouched posture, her arms defensively across her torso, awkwardly placed feet, her dull hair and the concealing overcoat. She is sitting on an uncomfortable kitchen chair. At the end of the piece, her hair has been done; her hands are in her lap; she is wearing much smarter clothes and sitting more comfortably in an armchair. Above all, her posture is upright, with some dignity and assertion of her presence. We can see that she now has more self-respect. Similarly, when Graham (*A Chip in the Sugar*) recovers his power, he makes the transition from perching on the arm of his chair or sitting on an unmade bed to being in an easy chair. Muriel's settings (*Soldiering On*) show her coming down in the world, and indicate the shrinkage of her world and possibilities. All this is immediately visible in the change from a comfortably furnished room with a brocade sofa to the same room stripped bare, and then to the boarding-house room at the end. Lighting is also used to indicate mood. All but one of the monologues end with 'getting dark', 'dusk', 'evening', 'night', whereas Irene's happy ending has daylight streaming in through the window behind her.

It is clear from Bennett's diaries just how alert he is to the way people speak, and how much his habit is to remember and record what people say, without comment or analysis. These diaries reveal the natural dramatist: the publication of such unglossed utterance suggests his conviction that such speech by itself can interest, amuse and illuminate. In the diaries are random bits of speech which we might overhear in the street, but they have been selected and emphasized by being presented to us for contemplation.

It is Bennett's ear for the registers of the spoken language which sets him most at a distance from the novel or short story and which enables him to root his characters in the world by indicating not only their origin (we hear the northern dialect and intonations) and gender (no man would talk like Muriel) but also their class and education. We know that Graham is more educated than his mother ('the rest of the operation devolved on me' against 'I never did'), that he reads *The Guardian* ('up-to-the-minute issues like the environment and the colour

problem') and is in touch with a therapeutic group ('a nice mix
personality difficulties as being the most fruitful exercise in problem-
solving'). This also avoids the monotony of a single voice, which a
monologue always risks.

Of the characters, Doris (*A Cream Cracker Under the Settee*) has
perhaps the most limited range of register, and Muriel (*Soldiering On*)
is consistent, but even in these monologues Bennett can use shifts of
language to highlight what he wants to signal. The ultra-respectable
Doris swears only once, and that is when she reports her fall ('oh hell,
the flaming buffet went over'). Irene's 'fuck' (*A Lady of Letters*) comes
as a surprise, but it signals release and companionship for her. There is
a marked change in Muriel's speech rhythms and sentence structure
towards the end, as though she can't bear to articulate fully and face
what has happened to her. 'Don't know why. Doesn't upset me. Miss
the tinies. Not so tiny, Lucy'll be twelve now. And twelve is like fifteen.
Married next. . . Not to be'. This is a long way from her fully articu-
lated, explanatory opening: 'It's a funny time, three o'clock, too late
for lunch but a bit early for tea. Besides there were one or two brave
souls who'd trekked all the way from Wolverhampton; I couldn't risk
giving them tea or we'd have had a mutiny on our hands.' Only at the
end does the fluent Muriel pause frequently, signalling something that
she dare not face. Doris's pauses frequently come after she has spoken
of her leg.

As with Susan and Geoffrey (*Bed Among the Lentils*), the balance of
power between Graham and his mother is mapped by the way one
voice's characteristic register swamps another. At first, they exchange
amicably: 'She said, "I wouldn't like you to think you're not Number
One." So I said, "Well, you're Number One with me too."' Graham
attributes his own idiom to his mother: 'She was in favour of stiffer
penalties for minor offences'. But when she meets Mr Turnbull, she
answers for Graham as if he were a child: 'He's between jobs at present . . . He used to do soft toys for handicapped children'; 'Oh he'll be
happy reading . . . Won't you, Graham?' She gradually assumes Mr
Turnbull's voice: 'A man shouldn't be living with his mother at your
age, Frank says'; 'Frank says it's the blacks', which drives Graham into
further withdrawal. He tries to talk about the situation in the therapeutic group, but, like Susan and her alcoholism, fails to. Graham feels
himself put down and disapproved of, fails to be heard and withdraws
home. When he breaks her relationship with Mr Turnbull, his mother
has a final moment of angry truth-telling, but in the end she assents to
their former mutuality: '"I do love you, Graham." I said, "I love you

, by being his echo once more: 'We could go to the
…ike old buildings, don't we, you and me?'

…ers frequently produce incongruity by shifting unexpect-
…e register to another, and Bennett is no exception. Graham
… 'Well, you're Number One with me too. Give me your
… will them'. Lesley 'can apply suntan lotion and read at the
same ti… That is what professionalism means'. Jesus was 'snotty' with
his mother; the altar is Geoffrey's 'working surface' and God is his
'chum'; Joy Buckle teaches 'Flowers in Felt and Fabric'. These are all
lines that will get a laugh – a response which belongs to drama rather
than to reading fiction.

Bennett uses this shift of register to ironize characters by implication.
We can recognize that Lesley is convinced she scores highly on all 'sections in the personality book' and has much to offer as a person and an
actress. But we recognize how stuck she is in clichés. Seven times on one
page something is 'interesting'; she continually asserts that she is 'professional'; she constantly uses people's first names, as do Graham's
therapy group, a habit which Bennett notices as a clichéd way of signalling relationship and support in his diary account of an Alcoholics
Anonymous meeting in New York. Her philosophical and psychological observations are pretentious clichés too: 'The day begins when
the day begins'; 'the something in me that was Travis had died'; Travis,
her character in the porn video, is 'a woman at the crossroads'. 'Is
Travis the type to go topless?' she muses. This is followed by a comic
and brutal shift of register: 'Gunther wants to see your knockers',
which undermines for the audience the whole edifice she has built up
about the film she is making.

'How're you coping?' Angela asks the bereaved Muriel, with her eye
on useful contributions for the charity she represents. 'Don't take
any big decisions . . . I don't see any shoes.' Geoffrey's parish group
produce 'gales of deep, liberated, caring laughter'. Graham goes to his
'Community Caring' and is thanked for 'sharing your problem with us.
Does anybody want to kick it around?'

It is not always easy to recognize whether or not the speaker shares
Bennett's ironic awareness. Is Muriel as well as Bennett ironizing
Angela, or Doris ironizing the midwife who, when her baby was born
dead, refused to let her see it: 'The midwife said he wasn't fit to be
called anything and had we any newspaper'? Graham appears to be
uncritical of the therapist's idiom, though he objects to being thought
'defensive about sexual intercourse'. He is defensive on the grounds of
not wanting to think of his mother as a sexual object – or a sexual

object to somebody else – not on the grounds of the assumptions betrayed by the phrase.

Susan is the only character who consistently and consciously uses the weapon of ironic incongruity. This makes her monologue one of the wittiest and an entirely appropriate one for the talents of Maggie Smith, from the initial phrase 'I'm glad I wasn't married to Jesus', to the closing one, 'problem wives whom they could do a nice redemption job on'. It is touching when for a moment she speaks of her lover without irony, that 'slim, flawless and troubled creature', and it is his concern about her drinking which finally makes her seek help, not that of Geoffrey, her husband, who brandishes 'We met it with love' like an 'all-purpose antibiotic'.

'As usual, I am struck more by who is doing the looking rather than by what they are looking at: worthy architects, with grey hair and bright ties, seeming younger than their age; pencil-slim architectural students dressed with casual care . . .; a lot of people who have probably had a decent salad for their lunch and come in their five- or six-year-old cars . . .' wrote Bennett of visiting a Lutyens exhibition. He is an observer, and he uses what he sees to type people and guess at other parts of their lives. Drama, more heightened and perhaps necessarily more simplified than prose fiction, thrives on types, and Bennett has clearly thought of them when writing some of the Talking Heads: he writes in the introduction that 'dozens' like Lesley have auditioned for his plays and films, and he generalizes about 'Lesley-like characters', 'their hopes', and 'these actors'. Doris is just such a recognizable type: she is on trial 'for not acting like a woman of seventy-five who has a pacemaker and dizzy spells'. Susan glumly acknowledges 'the hair, the flat chest, the wan smile, you'd think I was just cut out for God'. The quotation from Bennett's diary also indicates how much his imagination responds to visible specifics. What someone eats for lunch and the sort of car they drive can be deduced from the tie and the face as part of a personality and lifestyle.

Bennett uses the selected images on the television screen to suggest types to the audience, but he knows there are dangers in typing people. In *Writing Home* he reports a dream which made him acknowledge the snobbery of reading respectable clothes as indicators of character. He wrote in the introduction to *Talking Heads* that he was surprised to discover how frequently trendy vicars and social workers were his targets. Muriel has the painful experience of being re-typed by others. *A Lady of Letters* deceives us, as it deceives its main character, by playing on our own readiness to typecast. The couple living opposite her, who don't have tablecloths or curtains, shout at each other and play the radio loudly, do not look like desirable neighbours. Highlighted before each blackout is a fact that makes the audience think of child abuse – the 'kiddy looks filthy'; 'I heard it crying'; 'It never plays out', while its parents go off every night without it. But both the viewer and Irene are wrong and have misread the indicators: the child's bruises are a symptom of the leukaemia from which it has just died. The information is as much a rebuke to us as it is to Irene. Perhaps it is also Bennett's rebuke to himself, as he is also an observer of other people and a fabricator of stories – also written down – about them. However, what remains with the audience is his respect for these neglected characters, and how funnily and inventively he has used the monologue form.

6 Sunset Across the Bay

Sunset Across the Bay is a television play about northern life and, being the story of an elderly retired couple, it is also a play about northern death. It manages to be both scrupulously realistic and poetic at the same time. The carefully observed realism of events, characters, language and locations (Leeds and Morecambe) confronts the audience with the unremarkable lives of people who are voiceless because they are powerless politically, economically, and culturally, and also because they are old and belong to a dying way of life. They have remained largely unheard dramatically, at least while the stage was the main medium for drama. With its smaller visual range, the stage is more verbal than film or television. By using television's potential for what can be silently implied by situation and visual images, Bennett gives powerful dramatic expression to the feelings and experiences of characters who cannot verbalize their plight fully and whose pain it is to live and die marginalized and unheard.

The play is about Mr and Mrs Palmer, who usually call each other Mam and Dad. They retire from Leeds, where they have lived all their lives, leaving their old terrace house which is to be demolished, and go to live in a flat in Morecambe. They start on their new life hopefully, but soon find themselves isolated, and have nothing to do. Dad particularly misses work and becomes very depressed. There is an interlude in which their son visits them from Australia, and suggests that they come to live there, but they decide not to do so. Then the man has a stroke in a public lavatory and dies. It is a commonplace and minimal story but Bennett's handling of its structure gives it emotional power.

After an opening performance of 'We'll gather lilacs', the play begins with Mam and Dad lying in bed together, a situation that punctuates the play. The first section concentrates on placing them in the network of relationships which they are about to leave. Bennett's point is that they have people to talk to, and through these conversations he handles the exposition. In this part of the play, the audience learns that the area is rapidly changing as houses are destroyed and people leave. They also learn that Dad is going to retire and they are going to live in a flat by the sea, because they fancy a change and it is Mam's ambition to go there. The section ends, as it began, with them in bed.

The next part of the play covers their removal day. It starts with the removal men packing and the couple leaving. A council official boards up their house and they see a nearby terrace of houses being demolished as theirs will be. They travel by coach to Morecambe, explore their new flat, and are brought tea by their new neighbour. At this stage in the play, doubt and hope about the future are still mixed. As the section comes to an end, Mam asks doubtfully in the small hours whether they have done the right thing in coming to Morecambe. On the other hand, the journey is a small adventure for them: Mam uses the lavatory in the coach and reproaches Dad as having 'no spirit of adventure' when he refuses to try it; she overcomes her embarrassment at going into the lavatory in front of the other passengers because Dad says that they need not bother about what people think now that they have retired. Mam repeats this remark when they have tea at two o'clock in the morning. The section ends with them laughing together in bed.

Much of the play concentrates on three big events: the removal, their son's visit, Dad's death. But in the next section, just as important to Mr and Mrs Palmer is the fact that they have nothing to do and their lives are empty. Bennett has the problem of dramatizing lives whose defining quality is a lack of significant events, and of making interesting what the people experiencing it find boring. His solution is a series of clearly separated episodes, all of which illustrate this emptiness. Through these apparently unrelated episodes, he develops themes and feelings: 'mucky Leeds' comes to be regretted; their relationship worsens under pressure; finally their feelings are forced into words. The last episode in this section is a funny and terrible scene in an old folk's club, after which Dad refuses to go there again. There is nowhere left for him to go.

However, the characters are offered somewhere else when, in the fourth section, their son Bertram visits from Australia. Dad reassures him that they are all right, and they go on a happy expedition by car to the Lake District. In the end, all three walk on the beach and Bertram suggests that they come to live in Australia. Dad thinks it would be no different there than in Morecambe and Mam refuses. By now we know that death is the logical end of the story and the play. The episode ends with all three figures in the Morecambe seascape looking at the sun setting.

The last section deals with Dad's death. They go to a cinema to see *The Go-Between*, and he lags behind as they come out. Finally, he goes into a public lavatory to 'shed a tear' and does not come out again. After some time, Mam asks a passing man to go in and find out what has happened. Dad has collapsed alone in one of the cubicles. Then follows a scene at the hospital where a doctor elicits the information that there is nobody he can contact: they 'don't have any proper neighbours'. Dad dies and Mam leaves, walking alone down the long perspective of the hospital corridor. There is a last shot of her in bed, and the play ends with her walking alone by the sea. It is brighter than other, similar shots; the sky and sea are bluer, and she waves her hand at a woman they had talked to earlier.

Bennett continually works by means of what is unspoken. Repetitions wordlessly indicate what he wants the audience to pay attention to, and, like the refrain in a poem, increasingly gather changing feelings round themselves. The many shots of Mam and Dad in bed chart the move from their early harmony to their first argument, after which she turns away from him, to the last shot of her alone, on her own half of the bed, Dad's side empty. There are anticipations of and parallels to the main story-line. For example, a woman who has recently lost her husband and is sitting unoccupied in a shelter, a neighbour who has nothing to do but stare out of her window at them, and Mam saying that they do not know how long they have to live. There are many ironies in the first section. The only thing Mam thinks will 'take a bit of getting used to' is not going upstairs to bed. Her friend grumbles about the quality of life in cheaply built flats. Dad is not sorry to retire: 'I shall miss it a bit, but not a right lot.' Before their move they are busy, purposeful and capable: 'There's that much to see to.' Dad says that toads live to a great age because 'they never move'. They have no idea what retirement will be like and what is in store for them, but the idle observation warns the audience of future events.

Much of the play's emotional power relies on the silent suggestion of visual images. It is punctuated by shots of figures – often solitary – in a landscape. Dad stands in silent contemplation of an empty room just before they leave their old house. They sit together on the grey sea-front in the silence of denial when Dad is feeling ill. The figure of Dad in a seascape soon becomes familiar: a small, lonely figure in a huge expanse of grey sky, mud and the scanty water of low tide. These shots in particular suggest loneliness, bleakness and death: the sea is frequently a symbol for life, which these shots repeatedly exploit by showing Dad isolated from other people and walking on the emptiness left by the absent tide. Sunset, which they contemplate with their son just before he leaves them, and when they have admitted that there is nothing new they can do, is a simple metaphor for age and death, and Bennett uses it as the title of the play. The Lake District landscape belongs to their moment of pleasure in being together with their son.

Mam, less depressed, is not shown alone in a landscape until Dad has gone into the lavatory and died. Then the film has to convey time passing and her growing fear, without dialogue. She walks and sits, and there are two separate close-ups of her face, with different expressions. When the camera pulls back from her the second time, the light has darkened. The emotional climaxes are also without dialogue: both the moment when the body is found alone in the cubicle, and the long sequence from the entry of the doctor after Dad has died are silent. The screens make no noise as the nurse moves them; Mam says nothing when she sees the body, and neither does the nurse; Mam's light footsteps fade away as she walks down the long hospital corridor. There is nothing to be said. The camera can home in on detail which is important to the play and says what words cannot: as the day in the Lake District comes to an end, there is a shot of rain falling into a puddle – like the tears Dad mentions in his last words. Other shots offer ironic contrasts. On his first solitary walk, Dad goes past last summer's battered hoardings, advertising the manufactured gaiety of a fairground; Mam, waiting for Dad to come out of the lavatory, is seen against the entrance to Morecambe Pleasure Boats.

The silence is intensified by the fact that Bennett makes only occasional use of background music. A cinema organ, which must have been a familiar sound to Mam and Dad during their youth, plays songs like 'This is our lovely day' and 'We'll gather lilacs' at selected moments: as the coach bowls along towards Morecambe, when Dad takes his first walk on the beach, as the credit titles roll at the end. Our ears are so accustomed to background music in films that the silence is noticeable during other highly charged scenes. There is no music as Dad stands alone in the home he is leaving; as they walk around their new flat; when Mam waits in vain for Dad; during the hospital scenes; and when she walks on the beach at the end of the film. In these silences, some small background noises are emphasized: the tapping of the hammer as their window is boarded up; the occasional sound of the sea and seagulls as Mam waits alone.

The medium also demands an understated acting style. Bennett relies on the actors making silence eloquent in close-up shots. Harry Markham as Dad, the less articulate character, is particularly impressive. We can see his strain in the frown line between his eyes, and his mouth, clamped tight and curved downwards, betrays the feeling that he cannot bear to speak. The boarded-up windows of their old house echo his closed face. What is left unspoken is at the same time a problem and a strength of this acting style. The pathos of Dad's stoicism and inarticulacy is clear. But it is less certain how unhappy Mam is. Is she also a stoic, courageously masking her own pain in order to deal with his? Is she denying her own anxiety to herself? Is she genuinely less unhappy than he is? At the film's end, the brighter colours and the wave to the widow suggest someone more cheerful and less isolated than her husband, yet sunset awaits her too and she has now taken Dad's place as the solitary figure in a seascape. Does their son really want them to go to Australia with him or not? Bennett risks lack of clarity, but the film's strength is the kind of uncertainty and complex mix of possibilities that are true to real life.

Through these charged silences, Bennett makes the play point to different kinds of voicelessness. Mam and Dad have no political voice, and the sources of political power are absent from the play. Mam attacks the people who have big cars, live in fashionable parts of Leeds and 'get on the Council' as the real vandals. We do not see or hear them, but these are the people who have the power to demolish her home, her neighbourhood and her world. Their perception of her home as 'slums' does not match hers. Their lack of sensitivity to her feelings is shown when an official boards up the windows before they even leave. As they depart, there is a shot of a row of houses falling down and anonymous figures, faceless in the long shot, moving in. The coach travels through a landscape dominated by motorway. 'Leeds thanks careful drivers', reads Mam. 'What about everybody else?' The two of them do not have a car and neither has ever learned to drive. This is not a landscape that accommodates her. The changing economic power of the north, and consequently its changing voice in the country, are also obliquely suggested. When Dad leaves, the engineering firm he worked for has been taken over, and he was given his leaving present by somebody who did not know his name. 'Old Mr Whittaker would have been there,' he says, but now there is a different kind of business ethos. 'No wonder the mills are closing,' exclaims Mam, looking at a mini-skirted girl walking past. The effect of unemployment is shown through the way retirement affects Dad. The snobbery about manufacturing industry that has bedevilled England and undervalued people like Dad emerges when their new neighbour calls on them. Her nephew is on the 'management side, of course' and it is 'a great boon' that there is no industry in Morecambe. Mam expresses her feeling of powerlessness when she says, 'We've never had a proper choice before' when wondering whether they have done the right thing in moving to Morecambe. And a limited choice she has had, between Morecambe, Australia and a tower block on the outskirts of Leeds.

The demolished houses and the closing mills indicate that this northern world and its way of life and working patterns are ending. The play is another account of traditions being destroyed. The cinema organ was the sound of their youth. They reminisce about the war and reflect that the Primrose League and Empire Day have gone. Mam and Dad have lived all their lives in a social structure, with 'proper neighbours' in the old terraces where traditional skills like gardening and entertainment like the piano were valued. 'Mucky Leeds' it may have been, but they belonged there. They had friends and neighbours who vanish from the play after the first section, and their world shrinks to strangers. There were male and female friendships: Dad's face is open and animated when he talks to Arthur and shows him a toad hibernating under a flower-pot. They gossip in bed about a woman who scandalizes them. Now 'there is only us left out of everybody we knew on our street . . . I don't see a person to speak to'. They can find no place in the new world of motorways and tower blocks. They lose their old roots and cannot put down new ones. In fact, the new world does not go in for roots: Dad says the 'young ones' have 'no ties, no place. Nowt'. Even their eating patterns are old-fashioned: they are too old to try yoghurt; they make a *faux-pas* by asking for tea and bread and butter along with their dish in an Italian restaurant where only rolls are on offer. 'The past is a foreign country', we hear from *The Go-Between* during the scene in the cinema. 'They do things differently there.' Mam and Dad speak only its language and know only its customs.

Their time and culture lead to other forms of silence. The respectability which Bennett sees as central in the northern working class life of his parents' generation is basically a desire not to be seen or heard. Mam 'can't abide everybody wanting to know your business', and her desire to be anonymous makes for stress in their new flat. She whispers, 'This is poor tea', because she is embarrassed that her neighbour might hear her through the thin walls, or 'She'll wonder what's happening' when she and Dad laugh together in the small hours of the morning. Bertram shows signs both of his upbringing and of his newly acquired habits when he hushes his mother when she apologizes to the waiter for knocking a milk jug over. To apply for 'the supplementary' would be a disgrace for Dad. Mam's fear of what people might think is shown comically when she says that she ought to have scrubbed out the soon-to-be-demolished house before they left it. The stoicism that this habit generates is admirable, but also limiting. There is a moment of hope that some freedom might develop when Dad says on the coach that they need not bother about what people think now that they have retired, and his tightly shut mouth relaxes into a smile.

Their intimacy can breach some small taboos: they speak frequently of going to the lavatory. However, they are diffident about expressing feeling. The woman in the shelter thinks the sea is wonderful and that 'people don't think about it'. Mam and Dad do not know what to say and are silent. The woman is made ridiculous by the way she goes on, but she is right to wonder at it and that people don't notice or express the wonder: Bennett takes an ironic and ambivalent attitude towards her. Dad denies to Bertram that he and Mam are experiencing any problems. As he sits, facing and fearing sickness and death, neither the audience nor his wife know what is going on in his head: it can only be inferred. He is both admirable in his stoicism, and pathetic in his inability to share his anxiety.

Bennett makes eloquent use of their minimal language and their northern idiom. They are not inarticulate but their culture inhibits their tongues. Certainly they are intelligent, and when driven they can express a problem simply and succinctly: 'Well it's not a holiday. Holidays you've got to pack it all in. You've only got a fortnight and then you've got your work to go back to.' Through repetition in significant circumstances, Bennett can make phrases like 'trailing about' imply more of Dad's pain than they verbalize. Even idioms can be made to carry unspoken feeling. Dad's final words are that he wants to 'shed a tear'. He means that he needs to use the lavatory, but it is the only time he verbalizes his sadness, albeit unconsciously. 'You've gotten yourself a right job there', he says to a man who is working in a garden. Understood literally, he says that having work is something that a man seeks and achieves. In the poetic context of the play, trivial, realistic details have metaphorical meaning too. 'It doesn't feel like our bed somehow . . . It gets shaken up', is a voicing of how radically disturbed their lives have been by their move. That they are not in their familiar place and that it feels wrong is implied by Mam remarking twice that 'tea has a right funny taste here'. Dad says it is made from different water. The second time that Mam says it is immediately before she expresses her doubt about the move for the first time: 'Have we done right, do you think?'

Retirement brings another form of voicelessness, and the man and woman deal with it differently. Dad's work is central to his life. To express his sense of his own value, he twice says, 'I had six men under me'; that he is no longer in charge is how he images his loss. When he has retired and speaks to a working man, he finds himself ignored. He is not spoken to or listened to. His desolation when a working man puts on his hat and announces, 'Well, some of us have jobs to go to', is suggested by the cut to his solitary figure on the grey mud flats. In retirement he lacks male companionship and is irritated by being limited to his wife's company and concerns, and also by being classed with the 'daft old lassies' at the club, where there are very few men. He, not Mam, worries about money. He projects other anxieties on to what is his responsibility. He is the bread-winner, and she does the housework and shopping. Now he envies her because she has not had to retire, and sees life as easier for women. Maybe it is, but she is being envied for her limitations: she did not have what he has lost. Mam says that it is retirement for her as well. Though the wretched Dad denies this, she has a valid point. Her situation is different after retirement too. Perhaps it is less traumatic, but it is still a radical life change for her to move, to have her husband constantly with her and to feel their relationship worsening. She has the defence of domestic duties and of doing the social things that people expect, like sending postcards. Dad refuses such defences: he will not listen to her suggestion that he should read or get an allotment. As Beckett does with Winnie in *Happy Days*, Bennett suggests that Mam's defences are both an escape and a sign of courage. They are important, though Dad's rational attack on her postcards and letters to Bertram – 'What is there to tell him?' he asks – is unanswerable. Though they deal differently with the fact, retirement means that there is nothing to say about their life.

'We work all our lives,' says Dad. 'It's all leading up to this.' 'This' is the silence at the end of their lives, and death is the final silence. The play is finally about the loneliness of age and waiting for death. The condition of age is waiting, not knowing, as Mam says, how long you have got, or what awaits you. There is a comical and dreadful attempt by the man who runs the old folks' club to give a voice to the elderly. Two women give sermonettes, which are treated patronizingly and not attended to, and, even more shockingly, Bennett's parody of such homilies makes them not worth taking seriously. There is another shocking moment when the camera closes in on a giggling, speechless and senile woman. The reason why we feel that they could not have chosen to go to Australia is that by the logic of the play we know Australia would be no solution to the silence and loneliness that finally face everyone in that empty landscape.

7   The Madness of King George

Neither George III (*The Madness of King George/George III*) nor Toad (*The Wind in the Willows*) is silent or powerless – rather, they are privileged and loquacious. Nevertheless, in these two characters Bennett gives voice to something that is normally unheard.

One of the sources of comedy is outrageous behaviour. It is comic to see characters whose assumptions and actions contradict our social expectations and moral judgements, instead acting unashamedly out of self-interest, or other impulses which we have long been trained to suppress in the name of civilization. When Mr Collins proposes to Elizabeth in *Pride and Prejudice*, he is comic because the reasons he gives for marrying are so contrary to our sense of what such reasons ought to be. Basil Fawlty (*Fawlty Towers*) is comic because he behaves in precisely the opposite way to how we imagine a hotel owner should behave to his staff, guests and wife. Comedy gives its audience permission to relish characters who behave as most of us would not dare to: Fletch in *Porridge*, Alf Garnett, Steptoe, Falstaff, Sir Toby Belch are all characters who dare to express what we would normally conceal. In them we can enjoy the behaviour of characters who we would perhaps prefer to avoid in real life, and we can ignore the distress they might cause.

In Toad and George III, created in consecutive plays only a year apart, Bennett has produced two such characters. Ian Buruma, in the *New York Review of Books*, points out how alike they are. Each acts out what Bennett calls 'the back parts of his personality' and has to learn to conceal them in order to create a socialized self, a process which every child must go through. That Bennett's imagination connects them is evident from the common features of the way he dramatizes the mad king and the bumptious animal. But while Toad is a straightforward comic treatment of the theme and is the same sort of traditional character as Fletch, George III is a much more complex case. Bennett allows him to release his outrageous back parts, but at the same time does not allow us to relax judgement and feeling. For the King, the release is agonizing. For the audience, there is no enjoying the outrageousness. The result is another of Bennett's characteristic tragi-comedies.

The Wind in the Willows

In the introduction to *The Wind in the Willows*, Bennett writes that 'There is a Toad in all of us, or certainly in all men, our social acceptability dependent on how much of our Toad we can keep hidden.' This is explicit stating of the need to render parts of the self unspoken and the extension of the principle to everybody. The Toad in all of us, like the King, is dramatized as a character whose inherited privileges free him from many constraints. Toad has no parents, no duties and no need to work. However, the King, being a sober and dutiful monarch, carries out his duties when he is sane. Like a child, Toad has no social responsibility, and comedy allows us to enjoy him doing exactly what he fancies. For most of us, that is one of the fantasies about adult life that we had when we were children: 'When I'm grown-up I'll only eat ice-cream and cake.' (It was bewildering that grown-ups continued to eat porridge and cabbage.)

Toad's childishness is consequently brought to the audience's attention, although the King's is obliquely suggested by painful and humiliating images. Toad acts like a spoiled child: 'Didn't. Didn't. Didn't'; 'I don't care . . . Nobody wants to hear about my lovely adventures'. He has tantrums when frustrated. His whims and passing enthusiasms are easily gratified – he has only to think 'I want' and he gets. He has marvellous toys (a motor-car, a train and a barge) which really work and whose perfection of detail Bennett vouches for in the introduction. The comic world, where nobody gets seriously hurt, is like a child's: a battle is promised, but the danger is reduced to nothing when a cowardly soldier asks, 'If my mum sends a note is it all right if I don't come in tonight?'

Toad embodies that back part of the personality which knows itself to be the centre of the universe: 'It's the end of everything', he announces. 'At least it's the end of Toad which comes to the same thing.' The conventions of comedy allow Bennett to make the world serve Toad. He has escaped from prison and is wondering how to get home: 'And how convenient! Here's a train', he says as a train pulls up beside him. He is utterly self-centred and conceited: 'Who else could elude his pursuers in so daredevil a fashion?' The modesty and humility which Toad learns to assume (the King learns, he does not assume – it is impossible to assume sanity) are the opposite of what Toad is really like: they satisfy him because everyone thinks him wonderful.

Both Toad and the King have a domain which they come near to losing through the traits dramatized by their childishness. Both suffer the humiliation of losing their place in the social order. The tragic fall from a height is acknowledged in *The Madness of King George* by the parallels made with *King Lear*: the passages quoted from Shakespeare are not parodies – they describe the King perfectly. Toad's fall is dramatized only by the comic spectacle of him in the dock (where the magistrate constantly defers to him), in prison (where the gaoler's daughter, in what Bennett points out is a convention of comedy, organizes his escape) and his trying inexpertly to do a tub of washing. Toad parodies tragedy: 'Tragic. Tragic,' says Hedgehog Harold, seeing Toad masquerading as a 'touching invalid', not actually being one, like the King. In *The Wind in the Willows*, Bennett parodies another famous tragedy, Ibsen's *Ghosts*, when he makes Toad, running rings around Rat in order to get his own way, exclaim, 'I want the sun. Give me the sun, Ratty, give me the sun!'

The back parts of both the King and Toad are dramatized by obsessive behaviour. Like the King, Toad becomes physically restless, which appears as desire for speed and excitement. Toad even has moments which echo the King's violent outbursts: 'And whack 'em and whack 'em and whack 'em.' The driven, unhappy King suffers the agony of going mad and knowing it. The language of madness is also used for Toad when he goes beyond what is socially acceptable. Bennett says that a psychiatrist would 'diagnose' Toad 'as subject to violent mood swings'. Badger calls Toad's obsession with cars a 'sickness of the mind'; he drives his bathchair 'like a mad thing'. 'He is not himself', says Badger during the trial, echoing the very words which Bennett chose when exploring the lost self of the King.

Toad's obsessions lead to flight, but not from himself and not in terror. For him there is only a stylized and comic set piece in which he is pursued by all the people that he has tricked and upset during the play. Like the King, he has to be forcibly restrained and imprisoned by the society he has not adapted to. He struggles, and is stripped of his clothes by the very people who are his friends and protectors. But instead of being brutally tied up, Toad goes into a bathchair – voluntarily, in order to trick his friends and escape from them, much pleased with his own superior ingenuity.

Finally, Bennett dramatizes the unrepressed back parts of Toad by incontinent speech, similar to the King's, and Toad too has to learn not to speak. His father told Badger about the secret tunnel rather than Toad because 'what [Toad]'s not good at is holding his tongue', and

Toad has to acknowledge that he is 'a bit of a talker'. At the end, he wants to 'tell everyone the news' and make a long speech at the party about his experiences in order to be the centre of attention and win 'tumultuous applause'. As Willis does to the King, his friends oppose him with 'silence', which is repeated three times in the stage directions. 'If he is going to live here and be respected he must learn to fit in', says Rat. It is exactly the same message that Willis gives to the King. But Toad learns only to pretend silence and modesty. This being comedy, he is not asked actually to change at all.

The Madness of King George

The Madness of George III was first produced as a stage play in 1991 and shot in 1994 as the film *The Madness of King George*. The more spare, pruned film script and the visual suggestions of film images emphasize the themes more clearly than in the play. The film, set in 1788, starts by concentrating on George III as a family man and a king, on the relationship between his public and private life, how little privacy he has, and the tension between him and the Prince of Wales. It traces his developing madness, the attempts of the Prince to gain power through becoming Regent, the ludicrous and dreadful medical treatments he suffers, and his recovery after humiliating though apparently successful treatment by Dr Willis. The King recovers just in time to reach Parliament and prevent the Regency Bill from being passed. The film ends with the entire royal family going to the thanksgiving service at St Paul's, grouped together and waving to the crowd. They are an icon of unity and happiness – and a sly reminder to more modern times of the wedding of Prince Charles.

The film's basic premise is division in the self, not only between the front and the back parts of the personality, but between public and private selves. There is constant attention to the boundaries between the different parts. For the King's subjects, the boundaries between public and private life in the presence of the King are clear and governed by convention. Pitt leaves the King by backing down an immensely long corridor – an exit that is socially correct, but ludicrous to the point of being comic. A heavily pregnant woman cannot sit down in the King's presence. Consequently, there is a feeling of release and relaxation when he leaves: the courtiers flop exhausted into chairs and the Princes kick their shoes off; pages throw the crown round among themselves. The Prince of Wales, seeing an unsuccessful murder attempt made on the King, says as a private man to his brother, 'One would consider that almost as vexing.' Publicly, as heir to the sovereign, he says 'I was rejoicing, sir, that you are unharmed.'

For the King, the boundaries are more blurred, because he is seldom permitted privacy. When the King assumes the Garter, robes and crown in the opening sequence, we see Fitzroy kicking a toy belonging to the King's small daughter and the King comforting her in a fatherly way. However, the directions for the scene are that when the King 'picks up the reins of government, the genial family man [is] banished in favour of his testy, impatient, official self'. Their family life is difficult, because their life is so public. 'Can we never be solitary?' the Queen asks despairingly as she tries to soothe the distraught King. They do have their intimate and affectionate married life in their bedroom, but the King is generally on public display. He sometimes attempts to escape into being 'Farmer George', a simple working man. He really is interested in and knowledgeable about farming, but since it is still a role assumed in public he can never actually be private in it. When he recovers and faces Parliament he asks approval of his performance: 'How was that, lads?' The final scene shows the need for the family to seem happy for the benefit of the public. The same necessity of seeming will characterize the secret self.

Since parts of the self have to be kept separate, there is much emphasis on what is fit to be seen and fit to be said. The King's two equerries, Fitzroy and Greville, are deliberately contrasted. Greville is sympathetic: he develops an affection for the King and is kind to him in his illness; he does not keep his feeling for the suffering private man sufficiently separate from his official functions. The ironically named Fitzroy is cold. When the King recovers, it is Greville who is dismissed and Fitzroy who is promoted. 'To be kind does not commend you to kings,' says Fitzroy. 'They see it, as they see any flow of feeling, as a liberty.' The successful, like Fitzroy and Lady Pembroke, know when to turn a blind eye to what they ought not to see. That one does not look at the King is one of the first conventions of court life which Greville is warned about, but fails to learn.

In madness, these boundaries are breached. Going mad, the King speaks of his hatred of his son in public, but in contrast, at the end, when he has recovered, he controls himself. He speaks coarsely to the beautiful Lady Pembroke and makes a physical and sexual attack on her in public: 'Sir', says the Queen, 'we are in company.' That the Queen and Lady Pembroke, like the King, appear undressed when the King runs mad is a visual image of what is not fit to be seen in public. There are parallels between the banquet scene in *Macbeth* and the concert which the King disrupts: the private madness bursts through into a public celebration. It is comic and crazy that Dr Baker undertakes 'physical examination only as a last resort; it is an intolerable intrusion on a gentleman's privacy. With His Majesty it is unthinkable.' But the conventional boundaries are dreadfully breached later, when the King is tied to a bench and tortured by blistering, and more constructively crossed when Willis takes hold of him and looks into his eyes. This boundary is restored at the end, to Willis's professional pleasure. In madness, the King loses both the public and the private self, which the Queen knows and loves but cannot now reach. He ceases to function in both spheres when they are cut off from his secret being and the murky, back parts of the subconscious become dominant.

This secret part of the personality is separate from the social self, public and private. It is not identified with the self by others who know the social façade: 'He is not himself', says the Queen in the common cliché, as the King's madness worsens. The sick King recognizes the separation. He loses the public and private self ('Papa . . . has just lost himself', he says to his daughter; to Willis he says, 'You do not see me. Nobody sees me. I am not here'). Yet when he recovers, he describes his sane self as the seeming one and acknowledges the reality of the mad one: 'I have always been myself even when I was ill. Only now I seem myself . . . I have remembered how to seem.' Madness and loss of the social self came when he lost the power to seem. The public performance broke down and all that was left was everything behind the scenes, places in the self that are not fit to be made public. The King is asked by Pitt not to attend the concert because he 'is not fit . . . to be seen'. Bennett uses the contrast between the public rooms of the palace and the tiny dark cupboard in which the pages sleep to suggest this visually, as well as the more obvious darkness and claustrophobia. It is reinforced by images of the King, Queen and Lady Pembroke appearing publicly undressed, the most striking of which is the image on the cover of the film text: the King runs between two rows of formally uniformed guards, who stand stiffly to attention, completely subordinated to their public function, while he, in a loose, flying nightshirt with his arms spread wide, reveals the secret man which ought not to be on view.

The secret self is as unfit to be spoken as it is to be seen. The eruption of his madness begins as inappropriate behaviour and incontinent speech. Intimacy allows some taboo areas to be seen and spoken of: it is appropriate when the King and Queen see each other in night clothes in the privacy of their bedroom, and it is a sign of their intimacy (though a shock to the public, the audience) when he tries to relieve his discomfort by farting in her presence (although with an apology even here). Comedy also allows taboos to be spoken of lightly, and that one of the King's doctors has an obsession with faeces becomes a running joke. But we are appalled when the King, in soiled clothes, squats to excrete in public – his most humiliating moment in the film. Further, Bennett clearly identifies what comes from the mad King's mouth with the uncontrolled release of filth from his anus. He is incontinent at both ends: 'howling helplessly . . . he takes Greville's hand and puts it over his mouth to stop him talking, while clutching his incontinent behind'.

In other works of Bennett's, inarticulacy leads to powerlessness. But in this one it is the King's speech that is a symptom of his loss of power over himself: 'Sir, you are talking', says the Queen, identifying his illness. The first sign of his 'spirits' being 'agitated' is that he talks 'so fast it is almost nonsense'. Silence is associated with control over himself. He needs quiet: 'Be *still*, sir', says the Queen. Immediately, she holds his mouth closed, stopping it from pouring out a stream of deluded indecency which ought not to be spoken, and at that point he has an agonizing moment of lucidity: '. . . Madness isn't such torment . . . I talk and talk and talk . . . I have to empty my head of the words'. He is helpless before his own verbosity: 'I follow my words. I run after them. I am dragged at locution's tail', an image drawn from a dreadful form of torture.

However, it is eyes, not words, which are Willis's instrument to counter and heal the King's driven speech. He has to teach the King how to be silent, to speak only what is fit and not to speak what should be unspoken: 'Clean your tongue.' At first, the King is literally and forcibly gagged. Later, he 'allows himself' to be gagged after making a verbal attack, and we understand that he is internalizing control. When he has recovered, we can see him, though watched and warned by the Queen and Willis, controlling what he says to his hated son.

What emerges about the secret self when it is spoken? The obvious answer is the literal 'crap' and 'filth' with which it is equated, and this is borne out by his preoccupation with Lady Pembroke and his public attack on her. But that his suppressed sexuality is erupting ('The cork's too tight in the bottle') is a suggestion made by Thurlow. However, we are not likely to trust his judgement, and therefore it is likely to be a crude account of his trouble. The affection of the royal marriage is valued, not mocked or ironized, and no suggestion is made that not 'kick[ing] over the traces' is to blame. The secret man manifests in violence: the King tries to throttle the Prince; he tells the musicians to give the music 'a good whipping'; he tries to strike Fortnum, and slashes thistles. The secret self is associated with the flow of feeling which is reckoned a liberty in Greville. It is also a longing for a lost Paradise, which America represents to the King and which must not be spoken of. But the King's subconscious is not made of nameable qualities like lust, violence and anger – these are manifestations of it. It is to do with energy and chaos, and is dramatized by physical energy: the 'King in headlong flight' manifests it and the terror of being driven by it. He is 'gabbling' as it spawns and teems in his head. His incontinent mouth pours out language, fast and incoherent. The words that the King follows are the product of its activity but do not define or describe it. Bennett dramatizes the King's mind spinning and freewheeling by the means of jokes and word associations: 'Mutter will be the matter'; 'Assaults. And salts beside . . .'; 'There is a mist. Oh, the Queen, missed . . . doctortures doctormentors . . .'. Bennett uses his own creative and comic energy with language to suggest the dark energy for which there is no language. The film suggests the back parts of the personality as formless, anarchic energy.

Freud called this energy libido and Plato called it Eros. The King's private failure to control this energy is twice related, in a Shakespearean way, to his power over the nation. Of him, it is literally true that he cannot govern his country until he can govern himself. The play associates self-governance with restraint, silence and seeming. Willis represents positive control, in contrast with the Prince of Wales, who represents control of a negative, manipulative kind.

Willis teaches the King that he 'must behave' and what he must not speak. The therapy is a battle for power which Willis wins. Dramatically, he needs to have the force and stature to counterbalance the King's authority, anarchic energy and despair. Ian Holm's fine performance of the doctor is based on silence and the force of his eyes and face in close-up. He not only looks at the King; he outfaces him. The turning point in the film is when 'Willis's look stops him' from spitting out soup and the King obeys the doctor. He is the King's opposite, representing another England, unknown to the King. In contrast to the other doctors, he is non-Establishment ('Not a member of the Royal College of Physicians', as Baker says indignantly). He comes from the Lincolnshire fens, belonging to the provincial, non-literary, non-conformist tradition which produced hedge preachers and emphasized morality and will-power. (The King must 'strive . . . towards his own recovery'.) Willis is not in awe of the King or bound by hierarchy, but ready to breach the boundaries of etiquette and challenge the King with his powerlessness and need.

The film suggests that in teaching the King to control his behaviour and speech, Willis is acting like a parent socializing a child. The King's childishness is stressed – the soiled clothes and defecating in public are normally only seen in children. The King is told that he must learn to behave and do as he is told. The restraining chair that Willis straps him into looks like a child's high chair. Willis feeds him with a spoon and the King spits soup back at him like a naughty child. Willis, the adult, is 'unmoved' and offers him more. The King surrenders and swallows the next spoonful. It is a shift in power. When the King feeds himself for the first time, the watchers clap. At the end, Willis 'does not look altogether unhappy' when the King sends him away. The 'parent' is pleased that the 'child' is independent.

Willis's approach is behaviourist, and the process of healing is shown as humiliating and painful, and is riddled with ambiguities. The King is brutally handled, bound and gagged, made to submit. Does Willis cure the King or not? Did he recover spontaneously from porphyria? Pitt thinks that 'time has done you the service, sir'. Is it punitive and horrible or necessary? Is the King bludgeoned into conformity or does he rightly internalize controls? Is it freedom or slavery to be at the mercy of the flow of feeling? (It is interesting that the play is set in the same period that Jane Austen was in her teens: her early novel, *Sense and Sensibility*, explores a similar tension and the question remains one of Romanticism's legacies to us.) Mad or sane, the King is both powerful and powerless. Sane and powerful, he is willingly bound by the court conventions he has internalized, and he is forbidden by Pitt to speak of his obsession with America, an appropriate control which is necessary for the maintenance of his government. He is immensely privileged, yet can paradoxically say nothing. Mad, he is freed from these constraints, but loses his power, and ends literally bound to a chair in a horrible parody of being on a throne while Handel's Coronation anthem is played 'at full volume'. He recovers power over himself through a man who ignores and denies his power, breaching all the boundaries that hedge a king.

If this is true, the self is necessarily created by suffering, a tragic view. Bennett takes the dramatic risk of invoking *King Lear*. 'The King, cloaked and bearded now, looks like Lear' he instructs. For an audience, the parallel is first and startlingly made in the scene when the convalescent King, Willis, Thurlow and Greville read the reunion of Lear and Cordelia. Once the idea has been suggested, one realizes how many parallels there are: the King in his nightwear outside on the roof at night is like Lear in the storm; he is humiliated and physically stripped; he has a good servant; the child wishes to rule the father; he meets the shock of resistance. The parallels repeatedly allow Bennett to suggest and verbalize King George's feelings with a power forbidden to him by the realist conventions of the script. For an audience, it is very touching and a great relief to have the pain spoken so eloquently in Shakespeare's words. Tragedy has traditionally been about highly placed people, as their status magnifies the effect of their suffering. Willis comments that to submit to control must be particularly difficult for the King, so he becomes the extreme case of the loss of power and humiliation which power over the self paradoxically demands.

But the film does not end in the same way as *King Lear*, and *The Madness of King George* is not a tragedy. Thurlow thinks that if Lear's messenger had arrived in time 'it would all have ended happily' and had 'a much better ending'. Tate's version of *King Lear*, in which Lear and Cordelia are allowed to survive, was still in use in 1788, and Bennett allows the King to be his own messenger and arrive at Parliament in time for the happy ending. There are plenty of comic moments and witty lines, even though the comic devices themselves often darken into pain. We can enjoy characters behaving outrageously: 'Fine cluster there', says the King, looking at Lady Pembroke's breasts; 'Here, that's against the law', says the clergyman, 'I am the law,' replies Thurlow. But the King's outrageous behaviour declines into madness and suffering. When the doctors, broadly caricatured ('Good news! A foetid and a stinking stool'; 'Whether a man's water is blue or not is neither here nor there'), actually treat a sentient and suffering patient, their comic outrageousness changes into the ignorance and horror of eighteenth-century medicine, and we see blistering, paralleled by juxtaposition to amputation without anaesthetic. The comic gap between what is done and our expectations or common sense ('I discovered I'm Bishop of Osnabruck', says the Duke of Kent) is used to underline the thematic divisions between public, private and secret selves. The comic gap also darkens as the King's insanity worsens and the boundaries break down. It is not only comic when the film juxtaposes the wretched King with Pitt's bland public reassurances (how contemporary they sound) in Parliament. Bennett relishes verbal jokes and starts the text with jokey stage directions: the Prince of Wales is 'too old for her to wipe anything off his face (except the smile)'; the 'job specification' for being Prince of Wales includes 'the ability to kick your heels for half a lifetime'. However, jokes are later used to signal the King's disturbed mind freewheeling. Most of the laughter comes, not surprisingly, at the beginning and the end. As the King recovers, the tone changes and Bennett plays a game with his actors. He has Nigel Hawthorne (King George) remark that Ian Holm (Willis) is 'a hopeless actor' and that the mad King character is affecting because of 'the way I play it'. Some comic stage directions reappear. The end is not tragic: it is Tate's *King Lear* rather than Shakespeare's. But the comic restoration is shadowed by a glimpse of the King's fear, our knowledge of his later history and by the fact that the royal family's show of unity and happiness is put on for the benefit of the public.

Learning to silence what ought to remain unheard is a slow and humiliating process, as the King demonstrates. Bennett is too much of a psychological realist to end even *The Wind in the Willows* as Grahame ended the book. He will not allow characters to change themselves easily. Toad learns only how to pretend to silence and modesty and does not alter at all. Mole speaks for the audience of comedy when he wants the outrageous character to remain unchanged. He fears, like the audience, that it will be a little dull without the old Toad, and the audience is pleased to hear at the end that the old Toad is still in business and unrepentant: '. . . this way I get more attention than ever. Everybody loves me! It's wonderful!' In *The Wind in the Willows* this comic voicing of what should be unheard admits our desire for the libido not to be suppressed; the tragi-comedy of *The Madness of King George* dramatizes the agonizing and necessary process of learning how to keep it unspoken.

PART THREE

The Writer

8   The Writer in Disguise: 1

The Writer in Disguise

In 1985, Alan Bennett published a collection of five television plays to which he gave the title, *The Writer in Disguise*. This title is puzzling, since none of the characters has any ambition to be a writer. Further, 'the writer' is an ambiguous phrase. English idiom allows Bennett to mean both 'me, the writer of these plays' and 'all writers'. The characters whom Bennett calls writers in disguise certainly have many similarities to the persona that Bennett presents to the public, but much that can be said about them can also be said of writers in general.

In the introduction to *The Writer in Disguise*, Bennett identifies three figures as the disguised writer. They are Hopkins (*Me, I'm Afraid of Virginia Woolf*), Phillips (*One Fine Day*), and Lee, the Chinese waiter (*Afternoon Off*). There are two more very similar figures in other Bennett plays: Graham in *A Chip in the Sugar* and Midgley in *Intensive Care*.

Me, I'm Afraid of Virginia Woolf is about Hopkins, an English lecturer at a polytechnic. He begins in a doctor's surgery, suffering from a vague malaise: 'I'm not happy. I'm uneasy, uncertain of myself.' He moves on to scenes with his mother, a bossy lady and a splendid part for Thora Hird, and his girlfriend, Wendy, a yoga instructor and health-food freak with a nice line in soggy emotional clichés. Unenthusiastically, he agrees to spend the night with her, and then goes to his evening class on the Bloomsbury group. The class is mainly middle-aged people who are 'refugees from life', and a young man, Skinner, who is not. A photograph of Virginia Woolf turns out to have been defaced by 'a large pair of tits' and the picture of E. M. Forster by a moustache and cigar. The class attempts to find out who is responsible by taking them into Mr Trickett's class on Mechanical Drawing and Wendy's yoga class. Skinner, intelligent and indifferent to convention, suggests that the graffiti are a comment on what the writers lacked. At the end of the class, he asks Hopkins if he wants to go for a drink, but Hopkins refuses because he has promised to go home with Wendy.

Their time together is as comically awful as he had feared ('Other people got foreplay. All he got was *The Joys of Yoga*'). Hopkins eventually leaves her to go home. On the bus, he sees a couple kissing, and though he buries himself in his book the boy punches him for watching them. Unexpectedly, he meets Skinner, and they go to the hospital together, so the film ends in a similar place to where it began. This time, there is the hope of some fun and pleasure for Hopkins, as Bennett includes the suggestion that they are going to have an affair and that the film has been a 'love story'.

Afternoon Out begins and ends with a 'Cambodian or North Vietnamese' waiter, Lee, working in the dining room of an hotel. He speaks very little English, but wants 'to meet young ladies'. His colleague, Bernard, has arranged for him to meet Iris: 'She likes me. He showed her my photograph ... I have bought some chocolates', he says, uttering more than he does during most of the play. Bernard writes down her name and tells Lee that she works in a shoe shop and comes out at four o'clock. With time to kill, Lee wanders into the town and drifts into a men's club, where he is ignored, an art gallery, where the attendant stops him from sitting down, and a church, where a woman chats to him. He arrives at the shoe shop, only to be told that Iris has been dismissed. An assistant tells him that her father works at Batty's, so he goes there, being side-tracked on the way into a pensioners' concert in a church hall.

At Batty's, Lee is exposed to racial prejudice and suspicion of drug dealing and pimping, which it is doubtful if he understands. Even so, he is told that she is working at the hospital and leaves 'very sadly. England is mad'. He asks in a coffee shop where the hospital is, goes there and is taken for a voluntary worker visiting an old lady called Iris. His chocolates are distributed round the ward, and he is sent away in disgrace by the staff nurse because Iris is diabetic. He ends by 'dejectedly' going back to Bernard, who is in bed with Iris himself. We never find out if he really tried to put her in touch with Lee or not, and the play ends with Lee back on duty. *Afternoon Off* is a series of comic vignettes of life in the town, where Lee stands on the sidelines of a culture which he does not understand and which does not understand him. His dialogue is minimal: 'Iris?'; 'No. No.'; 'I want Iris' is all the text he is given in the five pages of the hospital scene, while the other characters speak loudly around him.

One Fine Day is set in a London estate agent's office. Phillips and his rival, a younger man called Rycroft, are trying to sell an office block that has been on the market for some time. Phillips is withdrawn, both at home and work. When his wife goes away to look after her mother and his schoolboy son, Robin, brings his girlfriend home to sleep with, he takes refuge by moving into the top floor of the empty office block. He seems happy to be alone with his tape-recorder, deckchair and the view of a young couple whose home he overlooks. He cheers up and begins to work more effectively. Rycroft discovers Phillips' refuge and decides to stay there himself in order to catch him and prove his guilt. Eventually, the chairman and a group of prospective buyers find Rycroft asleep in the building and he is dismissed. The building is sold, Phillips' wife returns, and he finds the courage to tell Robin that his girlfriend must go home for the night. The play ends with him feeling more satisfied with himself.

Phillips is very like Midgley in *Intensive Care*, a television film not included in the *Writer in Disguise* series. Midgley is another silent, glum, middle-aged man, unremarkable at his job, without much of a relationship with his wife and a schoolboy son who does not respect him. Like Phillips, he is constantly on camera but has little to say, and he also finds temporary escape and refuge, although with a nice night-nurse rather than in a bolt-hole. Like Lee (*Afternoon Out*), he feels a failure at the end. Bennett himself played Midgley in the film, and also Graham, the Talking Head of *A Chip in the Sugar*. Graham is an extreme case of this kind of character: withdrawn, isolated and incompetent about living.

Bennett recognizes how alike Hopkins, Lee and Phillips are when in the introduction to *The Writer in Disguise* he summarizes them as 'Passive, dejected, at odds with themselves'. He adds that this kind of character is 'doleful . . . whatever his get-up, he slips apologetically in and out of scenes being heartfelt, while the rest of the cast, who are invariably more fun (and more fun to write, too), get on with the business of living . . . But it's hard to find words to put into the mouth of the central character when "Gr-rr-rr" or "Oh dear" seem to say it all'. He does not go on to explain why he sees these figures as being like the writer.

One can add other qualities to Bennett's list. These characters are socially awkward and embarrassed, relating uneasily to other people. Hopkins spends his time in the doctor's surgery wondering whether or not to move away from the girl he is sitting beside. He uses books as a barrier so that he does not have to face encounters, and feels himself different from other people and not one of the human race. Phillips sits alone in a corner of his living-room, with headphones on, listening to music while the others watch television in a group, and is afraid to tell his son that he does not want him sleeping with a girlfriend in his house. Lee cannot converse with anybody. All three are lonely and isolated people who have very little fun.

Some are also emotionally and sexually immature: Graham is 'married to his mother' and still lives at home. 'Don't leave me, Mam', he pleads, when she announces she is going to remarry. Hopkins knows 'only too well' what it looks like to be 'not married at 35 and sat here with his mam'. Both men use the child's word 'mam'. Phillips and Midgley are married, though not very successfully. Hopkins, teaching Virginia Woolf, wonders whether some more exciting experiences would 'be any more Life than a middle-aged lady sitting reading in a garden', and answers himself, 'Yes. Yes. It would'.

Being lonely and isolated, they are spectators of life. When the young man on the bus punches Hopkins, it is for being a voyeur, somebody who watches other people relating closely in a way that he has failed to do himself. Phillips, high up and alone on the roof of the tower block, can see a little house on the roof of another building below him, where there is a couple with a baby. He too watches them kissing, and also observes his son kissing his girlfriend. Lee is the clearest case of the alienated spectator. A foreigner with minimal English, he is desperate to make human and sexual contact, and the play is a catalogue of his attempts to find it in a society totally inexplicable to him. He is not part of the world of the play and can do nothing but watch and try to make sense of what he sees going on. The failure of his attempt to do so constitutes the meat of the play. Bennett writes in the introduction that the film unit found a marvellous old snooker room in a men's club and the director asked him to write a scene so that it could be included. That a scene could be written simply to include a good location clearly indicates how external Lee is to this (or to any) situation. The characters in it ignore him, and he watches the action, just as we do through the camera's eye, and he fails to take part in it.

It is easy to see why Bennett thinks these characters are less fun to write than others. There is a moment in *Me, I'm Afraid of Virginia Woolf* when the caretaker comes in and scolds Hopkins for leaving his classroom untidy. Hopkins' response is apologetic, unconfrontational and deferential: 'O dear', as Bennett puts it in the introduction. Skinner is the character in the play who attacks back with energy and wit. The writer's playful imagination and his verbal inventiveness go into Skinner's demolition of the caretaker. We laugh at Skinner's wit, but if we laugh at Hopkins, it is at his absurd ineffectiveness. Midgley and his awful Aunt Kitty contrast in a similar way: he is silent; she has the funny lines.

So why are these people seen as 'the writer in disguise'? Taking 'the writer' in its sense of 'the writer of these plays', they share some of Bennett's own public persona: his – actor's – voice is usually glum, his face deadpan, and he rarely smiles when performing. He presents himself as mild, respectable and conformist. (There is 'some of wanting to please the teacher about me', he writes.) He says that when he was an adolescent, he was, 'Shy, bespectacled and innocent of the world . . . I'd never even been near the fire'. He reminds us of his modest background, and certainly sees himself as not normally free to be outgoing. When filming, he says, he is freer to chat with members of the public, having 'a setting and frame of my own'; sounding as if he normally feels insufficiently anchored in a social group. However, Bennett admits 'I am more gregarious than I like to think.' 'I have very little knowledge of "ordinary life",' he claims. 'I imagine it in a script and come up against the reality only when the script gets filmed . . . I imagine someone could be educated in the same way by promiscuity.' In *The London Review of Books*, he writes, 'I get pleasure out of being able to do simple, practical jobs – mending a fuse . . . – because these are not accomplishments generally associated with a temperament like mine. I tend to put sexual intercourse in this category too.' Like Larkin, he creates another role for himself as sexually awkward.

Of course, his audience and readers cannot know how like the real man this recurrent character is. Bennett may have acted Midgley and Graham, but he certainly is not like his fictional characters in his linguistic elegance and fluency, his command of attention and audience, let alone his success and versatility. None of the 'writers in disguise' has his wit or inventiveness or looks at the outside world so alertly and with such clear, amused and compassionate eyes. But nevertheless, Bennett has said that there are points of resemblance between them and 'the writer'.

Taking 'the writer' to mean writers in general, just how much do they have in common with every author? Writing is a lonely thing. The writer has to separate himself or herself from people to do it, withdraw into their own corner of the house and, like Phillips, metaphorically put their headphones on. It is not simply passive, but it does mean withdrawing from the normal business of living for a time. 'Living' is precisely what Midgley and Hopkins feel that they are not doing, and they say so frequently. At moments, Bennett himself says, paraphrasing Larkin: '. . . life is generally something that happens elsewhere'; and 'I suspect that Hopkins's "O my pale life" is me presenting an edited version of my own'. He makes his Hopkins blame his discomfort on his habit of putting himself in the place of other people, which is precisely what any good dramatist has to do.

It is surprising to find the almost totally inarticulate Lee offered as a representation of a writer, often the most verbally gifted kind of person. He is in the same situation as a writer in his isolation from the rest of the world, trying to make sense of it, and communing with his own thoughts, rather than other people. His unhappiness therefore suggests the writer's.

Like Hopkins, Lee and Phillips, the writer is an observer: '. . . an onlooker, which for much of the time I am', says Bennett of his own experience. To be a truthful and accurate observer, to pay scrupulous attention to the world, is virtuous, at least for a poet like Keats or a moral philosopher like Iris Murdoch, and the writer's moral function is to report such truthful observations. But the observer is necessarily separate from what he observes. Loneliness is necessary for his proper function. Bennett is scrupulous, observant and truthful, interested in the humdrum and ordinary, and believes that 'accuracy of dialogue and precision of observation' will do half of a comic writer's job for him without the need for contrived jokes. But *The Writer in Disguise* suggests that the brilliant combination of truth and comedy in his work costs an author separation, loneliness, unhappiness and feelings of not living. It also costs guilt, as observer easily becomes voyeur, as Hopkins and Phillips literally do.

Literature in these plays is as irrelevant and impotent as the characters feel themselves to be. Graham and Midgley, who, like Hopkins, teaches English, are highly educated, and not much happier or more competent as a result. Hopkins is the fullest treatment of a man professionally soaked in literature. As he worries about sitting beside the girl in the surgery, the voice-over reflects, 'Life . . . was full of such problems and literature was not much help.' When Skinner suggests that the defacing of the authors' photos is an appropriate comment on their shortcomings, he seems to suggest that their lives and their books betray sexual inadequacy. Trickett, teaching maths to the young unemployed, says quite rightly that literature and art alone cannot deliver his pupils: only their Higher National Certificates can. Skinner comments on the elitism of Bloomsbury: 'If Virginia Woolf had been born in Brighouse she'd never have got off the ground.' And when one of Hopkins's class says sentimentally that Woolf's novels were her children, Mr Dodds disposes of that by a disillusioned account of what it really means to be a parent. Skinner asks Woolf's photograph, 'Was it worth it?' The play certainly does not say that it was.

Though Bennett has acknowleged, by the title of his book, that there are analogies between one of his recurrent character types and the writer, he has indignantly denied a much more obvious connection between the writer and another of his characters, Ms Craig in *Enjoy*: 'James Fenton . . . even referred to the drag character as "the writer". Mr Fenton's subsequent abandonment of dramatic criticism to become the *Independent*'s correspondent in the Philippines was one of the more cheering developments in the theatre in the eighties'. In spite of this warning, given the character, one could be forgiven for tentatively suggesting not identification but some analogies.

The analogies between Ms Craig and the writer are obvious: she does not participate, but observes and writes down what she observes. When she arrives on stage, she goes instantly to the edge of the stage, takes out a notebook and begins to make notes. She has a soliloquy at the end of Act 1, but enters into no dialogue with other characters until the last quarter of the play. She has intimate knowledge of what she writes down, since these are her parents and this was once her home, but she is detached, since she left them long ago and has changed so much it is as if she had changed gender. There was ambiguity over whether *The Writer in Disguise* was meant generically or autobiographically. Here, there are clear autobiographical parallels between Bennett and his character: Ms Craig left Leeds, took a degree at Oxbridge, settled in London and joined the middle class. Like Bennett, she revisits her roots and writes about them: 'I wanted to refresh my memory. It's my job', she says. She wants to recreate the way of life she knew as a child for the entertainment of the paying public. Bennett, in his TV plays, has done just this.

Further, she is the character who invented the plot. As the play reaches its climax, she brings in a team of technicians (with clipboards and camera) to execute her idea. One of these technicians behaves like a film director: he ignores Mam and Dad except as effective props ('He maybe runs his hand over Mam's face absently'; 'the flesh is so good: white, white, *white*') and concentrates on whether the house has the right image ('The mantelpiece is perfect'). Later, the technicians carry off walls and furniture. They are dismantling both the house which is being taken to the theme-park and, at the same time, the stage set of *Enjoy*. The stage image suggests that the theme-park house will be Ms

Craig's production, as the stage house is the production of the imagination of Bennett and the director of the play.

The presence of discomfort is betrayed by the way Ms Craig deals with her material. Though Mam denies that they will be like animals on show in the zoo, Dad rightly feels 'condescended to' and the 'director' sees them as 'disappearing tribes'. It is comic and shocking when he treats Mam and Dad as props with which he can produce a 'powerful image', ironically an image of 'genuine community' where warm, familiar neighbours will bring consolation. 'Genuine' will be the last thing that this artificial community will be. This is comically emphasized by the line that says soot will be falling 'on certain appointed days'.

The episode which most tellingly dramatizes the guilt of the observing writer's detachment from his material is when Dad is visited by a young delinquent, accompanied by Gregory, his silent observer. He brings with him one of the pornographic magazines that he and Dad usually look at together. This particular one carries a photograph of Dad's daughter, Linda. When Dad refuses to recognize her, the youth threatens him. Ms Craig and the other observer stand up when Dad appeals for help, but do not stop the youth from striking Dad on the head. The attack leaves him paralysed, incontinent and helpless. '. . . and her just sat there . . . She sat there and watched', says Dad later. Mam refuses to believe that 'another human being' would do nothing, but we have just seen for ourselves that she did exactly that. Ms Craig and Gregory are guilty of standing by, observing inhuman behaviour and doing nothing about it. It is where being an observer becomes culpable, and it is the source of the writer's guilt which Bennett admitted to in the preface to *The Writer in Disguise* and which he examines at length in *The Insurance Man*. Interestingly, after the stage direction, 'Gregory and Ms Craig rise', Bennett gives no directions about what they should do or about when they decide not to interfere and sit down again. It is almost as if his imagination shrank from filling in the blank. Later, Gregory speaks an appalling line: 'The bugger looks dead to me.' The text gives Ms Craig no reply and no reaction.

Further, the play insists that Ms Craig, the recording observer, inevitably distorts her material, so that it can never be genuine. 'Go away and I might be natural,' says Dad. 'Me alone in a room. What's that like? You'll never know.' This is repeated in 'You distort things, watching, sitting there', and developed fully and farcically when Dad is thought to have died. Mam fetches Mrs Clegg, their neighbour, who brings her observer with her. Because she is being watched, she puts on an act of being a neighbourly tower of strength. The point is made that neighbourly help with the archetypal ritual of washing the corpse is just a show put on to please the observers, and Dad's involuntary response is a memorable refusal to join in. In the confusion that follows, Mam tells the observers just how few of the old traditions Mrs Clegg actually keeps alive.

If the presence of the observer inevitably distorts the situation, the comic dramatist is likely to distort it even more. 'Tie it down. Tether it,' says Mam, in a moment of wild comic invention. In another scene, she says, 'They're writing all this down and none of it's normal. Cocktails in a Rolls Royce. Linda flying off in Concorde and now Dad dead.' It is the comic dramatist who makes this unlikely scenario happen to Mam and Dad. 'You're lucky to have had such an action-packed day,' replies Mrs Clegg. The dramatist has to invent action, and pack enough surprising and amusing events into his play to keep the audience entertained.

Bennett again identifies observer and voyeur, but this time with much more distaste than he did in *The Writer in Disguise*. When Linda brings Heritage into the house, they find the presence of the impassive and silent Ms Craig sexually stimulating: 'I want to see you, seeing her, seeing me,' he says before they come close to 'coitus on the carpet' in front of her. Later, Dad pleads with Linda to take him with her, offering himself as a useful stimulus to her clients: 'Some people like being watched. Being watched improves it for some people.' The activities of voyeur, sociologist and writer are here seen with distaste as kindred kinds of perversion.

There are enough parallels between Ms Craig and 'the writer' to suggest Bennett's unease about a writer's relationship to his material. His nostalgic wish to celebrate and re-create the past in fictions may lead to sentimentalizing and misrepresentation, and his necessary detachment could be a sort of perversion and a refusal of responsibility to the real world. *Enjoy* is set in the same world that Bennett has written about so touchingly and funnily in his television plays. The initial situation is like that at the start of *Sunset Across the Bay*, but this stage play is handled quite differently. It is anti-realistic, more farcical, and much darker, with moral guilt and ambiguity, as it highlights the presence of the writer, that observer with the notebook.

9   The Writer in Disguise: 2

Single Spies

There are other characters who are lonely and who occur in Bennett's plays; these are the upper-class Englishmen who choose the isolation and detachment of the spy. They are Hilary (*The Old Country*), Burgess (*An Englishman Abroad*) and Blunt (*A Question of Attribution*). It is worth asking if the last two especially have anything in common with 'the writer'. Bennett is ambivalent about the Burgess character, particularly regarding his power to entertain and seduce an audience, and this suggests reservations about the same gifts in the writer. *A Question of Attribution* dramatizes another form of ambivalence: the way in which artists and their works of art simultaneously invite and resist investigation and interpretation.

An Englishman Abroad (stage version)

An Englishman Abroad exists in a television version, which was broadcast in 1983, and a stage version which, along with *A Question of Attribution*, was performed as a double bill, *Single Spies*, in 1988. It is based on an encounter between the actress Coral Browne and the spy Guy Burgess in Moscow. Burgess invited Coral (as she is always called in the play text) to his flat so that she could measure him for some suits and arrange for them and other clothes to be sent to him from England. The final exchanges are between Coral and a tailor, who accepts her order without fuss, and a pyjama-maker, who refuses it and turns out to be Hungarian.

In his introduction, Bennett explains what interested him in Coral Browne's story about her encounter with Guy Burgess: 'The picture of the elegant actress and the seedy exile sitting in a dingy Moscow flat through a long afternoon listening again and again to Jack Buchanan singing "Who stole my heart away?" seemed to me funny and sad.' Incongruity is a source of comedy because, looked at from the outside, it is surprising and absurd. It is also a source of pain because it creates tension and confusion when experienced from within. The presence of incongruity in Bennett's play is what makes it tragi-comic; he is a dramatist who has both a sympathetic identification with his character and enough critical distance from him to use comedy, outsider and insider at the same time. Burgess has exactly this kind of attitude to England: he is an insider, retaining the habits and love of a country which he has critically detached himself from to betray. This incongruity attracted Bennett, and suggests some analogies between the spy and the writer.

The stage image with which the play starts is 'A projection screen hides the set . . . and projected on it is the head of Stalin as we hear a record of Jack Buchanan singing . . .' This odd mixture of stylish entertainer and political tyrant sets the audience a puzzle: what connection can there be? Here is an initial example of the incongruity which is Bennett's theme. We find later that Coral belongs to the theatre world – in fact, she was once engaged to Jack Buchanan – and Burgess belongs to Stalin's world. But the split is not a simple one: Burgess loves the elegant English singer; he owns the record and plays it repeatedly, so the incongruity – which is certainly funny – is within him as well as between him and Coral, and his nostalgia is sad. He is a man living with the pain of two contradictory values, holding on to and missing what he has chosen to turn his back on. Burgess's first monologue dramatizes this incongruity. Comically, he does *The Times* crossword, the *Statesman* competitions and reads Trollope and Jane Austen, the most English of writers. His cultural world is still English yet, to him, England is now 'the outside world' and he lives inside Moscow. He calls himself a 'gentleman of leisure', a phrase implying the kind of person Austen or Trollope writes about, but he uses it to describe his empty life in Russia. He comments that Stalin's death 'cheered [one] up no end' because he suddenly had 'something to do'. The sad boredom and waste betrayed by this echoes Bennett's phrase from the introduction, the 'long afternoon'.

When Coral meets Burgess, she sees he is 'English . . . upper class and . . . drunk' and, as the play goes on, his Englishness is emphasized: he sings Church of England hymns and Gilbert and Sullivan songs ('He remains an Englishman', of course, from *HMS Pinafore*). From his conversation with Coral, we find he knows *Hamlet* and plays the English game of disrespect for cultural monuments. He once lived in Jermyn Street; his gossip and acquaintances were the English intellectual establishment – Connolly, Auden, Pope Hennessy, Harold Nicolson (comically, it is the exile in Russia who knew them; Coral

[99]

does not); Moscow is like Cambridge in the Long Vac: boring. Again, the incongruity is funny, but it is sad that he still draws imaginatively for his playful simile on the country and class which he betrayed and is exiled from. He wants English upper-class, tailor-made clothes, shoes, pyjamas and an Old Etonian tie, and would like some English false teeth; he makes the jokes of an English insider (a scrounger is 'a real Queen Mary'); he does not speak Russian, and calls Maclean, who does, by that schoolboy taunt 'swot'; he loves England, and like Hilary, the spy and exile in *The Old Country*, he does not want it to change.

Yet Burgess has an outsider's detachment as well. He knows England's weaknesses: it is 'timid, tasteful, nice'; it is made uncomfortable by 'unconcealed appetite' (embarrassment is something that Olga in *The Old Country* and Coral in this play both identify as English); it is not interested in ideas. He does not like 'the system' (how he answers Coral when she asks him what Moscow has to offer): he has been alienated enough from England to betray it, to tell its secrets and finally to go into exile in another society in which he still finds himself an alien. In Russia, he has to stay at home each day for a phone call to check on him; he does not know if his boyfriend is a policeman or not; he does not speak Russian. Here he is simply 'the Englishman', the outsider, stripped of the charm and privilege that his language and class would have given him at home. There is a moment in the play when Coral misreads 'a gent' as 'agent'. This is witty because the two should be incompatible and are actually identical, but the simultaneous identity and incompatibility perfectly describe Burgess's lonely and painful situation. Towards the end of the play, Burgess is reported by Coral as weeping: here is a sophisticated and highly verbal man suffering from the same alienation as Lee, the inarticulate waiter in *Afternoon Off*.

Burgess is also presented as a performer, who uses his eloquence to disarm and seduce. He has charm and a gift for language, jokes and entertaining people. But Bennett is also uneasily aware that these gifts can be used to seduce; quite literally, to get away with murder. 'Hungarian' is a reminder not only to Coral but to the audience that the character who has made us laugh and feel sad has helped to support a regime which committed murder, and the play entertains us partly by treating his action as a 'minor social misdemeanour'.

The parallel between theatre and the situation in Russia is presented attractively and wittily in Coral's opening monologue: 'Stalin died in 1953. I was in *Affairs of State* at the time, a light comedy that had a decent run at the Cambridge. Stalin had had a decent run too, though I'd never been a fan . . . After Uncle Joe's death they played with the understudies for a bit, then brought in a cast of unknowns in something called *The Thaw*.' Affairs of state are ingeniously paralleled to light comedy and this is how *An Englishman Abroad* promises to develop.

We know from the start that Coral is an actress but, in another sense, Burgess is an actor too. It emerges that he directed plays at Cambridge and he now wonders how he might have fared in the theatre. And, he says, as a spy 'I was a performer': it was how he got away with it. He explains that he 'wore a mask', pretending only to be exactly what he was. In other words, his colleagues believed him to be only acting his role as Marxist, while he was in fact being one as well. His costume and make-up were the ways in which he conformed to English tastes and habits: 'How can he be a spy? He goes to my tailor.'

Coral's description of their meeting tells of him vomiting drunkenly and repeatedly in Michael Redgrave's dressing-room. In their first passage of dialogue, she discovers that he also stole her soap, Scotch, cigarettes and face powder. Burgess is shameless, and he gets away with it through charm: he is a seducer and he knows it. 'I always had charm', he says. Coral recognizes that she is being milked and manipulated: 'You still have charm. She said through clenched teeth.' 'For charm one needs words', says Burgess, meaning that in exile he is powerless because he speaks no Russian. 'Sex needs language,' he says, making the association between seduction and linguistic gifts. His charm, his capacity to put on a seductive performance, come from his gift of words, and his wit. Immediately after acknowledging all his thefts, he comments on the concierge on the door: 'I'm always struck by her pronounced resemblance to the late Ernest Bevin. They could be sisters.' 'Brothers' would be mildly funny; 'sisters' has much greater inventiveness and absurdity, and here, the audience is being seduced too. It takes reflection afterwards to produce a moral judgement on him and his actions. Watching the performance, we just enjoy him – the usual response to the lovable rogue like Shakespeare's Autolycus in *The Winter's Tale*, or like Parolles in *All's Well that Ends Well*, another problem comedy, with a character who is also unmasked as a traitor. Coral's response parallels that of the theatre audience, and Burgess parallels a witty comic writer in passages like this: a writer in disguise.

Burgess relishes and values wit. His objection to Maclean ('Maclean's not my friend . . . Oh no, not Maclean', he says emphatically) is 'He's so unfunny, no jokes, no jokes at all.' He then continues with a joke: he resents being paired with Maclean like 'Crosse and Blackwell, Auden and Isherwood'. He has a way with understatement: 'I have only one suit. It's the one I came away in and I've fallen down a lot since then.' He plays with possibilities, like a writer. Of his friend Tolya he says, '. . . I'm not sure whether I've found him or been allotted him. I know what I've done to be given him. But what has he done to be given me? Am I a reward or a punishment?' Burgess imagines a chunk of the Communist Manifesto being written into the Queen's Speech and nobody noticing. He has a gift for anecdote and comic climax: for example, his account of the English ambassador's advice to him about how to behave in America (not being left-wing, avoiding the colour question and homosexual incidents). He summarizes this neatly as 'Don't make a pass at Paul Robeson'. When Burgess is on stage, he is the centre of attention and the source of wit, while Coral serves largely to feed him lines, though Bennett gives her entertaining monologues when she holds the stage alone.

Coral is the audience to Burgess's performance. He asks if he is boring her – the basic question every comic writer wants to ask his audience. She says to him the kind of things we would like to say. After he has repeatedly shown his Englishness and alienation from Russia, she asks him what he has gained by his spying and exile. She speaks for the audience again when she says, 'You pissed in our soup and we drank it' and '. . . we have sat here all afternoon pretending that spying . . . was just a minor social misdemeanour . . .' The Australian actress challenges the English attitudes of the spy; the audience might also challenge the English attitudes of the play in just these terms, because that is exactly how Bennett has treated the crime so far. He has written the play with the ironic habit of mind which characterizes the English insider. But Bennett, in writing Coral's speech, is also challenging the audience, who have so far accepted and enjoyed the dubious terms he offered. Coral declines moral judgement. What she resents is being taken in, manipulated, made a fool of; 'conned' is her word. As both she and the Foreign Office were seduced by the spy's charm and wit, so the audience has been seduced by Bennett's into seeing Burgess – traitor, thief and manipulator – as funny and sad. That Coral recognizes this is a form of seduction is clear in her sexual metaphor: 'Pipe isn't fooling pussy'. She speaks for the audience yet again when she asks him why he did it. His reasons once again suggest the writer's: a desire for solitude and a desire to tell, a paradox wittily worded: 'No point in having a secret if you make a secret of it.' At the end, Coral vigorously attacks the pyjama-maker's refusal to supply her with pyjamas for

Burgess as English hypocrisy. He replies, 'As a matter of fact, madam, our firm isn't English either.' When she asks what it is, he replies, 'Hungarian'. The play is set in 1958, two years after the Hungarian uprising, and the shock of that challenges the audience as well as Coral. It could also be seen as Bennett's challenge to his own powers of seduction.

Some viewers have found Bennett's Burgess superficial and morally contemptible and wondered why Bennett found him interesting. Certainly, Bennett refuses to condemn him morally, and finds him more 'likeable' than Blunt. Dramatically, he is more sympathetically presented than the cold Blunt or the destructive, defensive Hilary. Perhaps one reason why Bennett found him more likeable was that he heard the story from Coral Browne in person and she, who had the most cause for outrage, had felt pity instead of anger, and had talked about him in ways which made him particularly congenial to Bennett's imagination and fruitful for his art. It is possible to feel much more judgemental towards Burgess than Bennett appears to, but 'Hungarian' does admit that the spy has moral charges to answer after all. At the heart of *An Englishman Abroad*, there is a tension between the way in which Burgess can be judged and the way in which he may be excused from such judgement by the seduction of Bennett's tragi-comic art. It is even possible to speculate that Bennett might have felt uneasily that he had traded on his own wit, charm and engaging self-deprecating public persona, and that it too is a con.

If, as I have suggested, the relationship between Burgess and Coral reflects the relationship between Bennett and his audience, it is worth asking if any other features of the spy reflect the writer. Bennett, like Burgess, is a performer and entertainer (Burgess's wit in the play is Bennett's invention). Bennett was attracted to writing about both George III and Kafka by reading a joke that each had made. Lindsay Anderson, directing *The Old Crowd*, objected to 'some of the jokes with which Alan, being so good at them, would compulsively pepper his dialogue'.

Like Burgess, Bennett is both insider and outsider: he loves England (he says in the introduction that he has put his own sentiments into Burgess's mouth) but is intensely critical of its faults and has betrayed it in play after play by telling what it is like. Indeed, Bennett's scepticism is more complete than Burgess's since he cannot believe that there is anybody to whom it would be worth betraying his country. But, like Burgess, Bennett wishes to share his secrets. As he says in the introduction, '. . . to conceal information can be as culpable as to betray it', and a writer's job is, after all, to tell and to get himself listened to.

Bennett criticizes England through Burgess and Coral, though with nothing of the sharpness of his attack on it in *The Old Country*. However, the tone of the criticism marks him as English, a paradox embodied in all his three upper-class spies. In the introduction to *Single Spies*, he says that 'an ironic attitude towards one's country and a scepticism about one's heritage is a part of that heritage'. It is one of the traditions of comedy to make the criminal a lovable scamp, and Bennett has written a play that in a very English way gets comedy from turning treachery into 'minor social misdemeanour'.

He also makes Coral challenge this attitude, as he has a moral objection to the status quo and needs to test his own culturally ingrained ways of thinking and feeling, and in this too he is like the spy. But Coral's criticism is challenged in its turn. Like Burgess, Bennett remains unable to settle for one side or another, inside and outside at once. This is another occurrence of the constant tension in his work, and echoes the tension between his northern childhood and his southern university life. There is a difficulty in finding a voice, a stance, a position, which will do justice both to the love that insider feeling brings and the distance which comes with intelligent detachment. Bennett's touching tragi-comic balance is his aesthetic and dramatic solution, and the figure of Burgess, delicately poised between being funny and sad, suggests the cost of that balance.

A Question of Attribution

Blunt, the upper-class spy in the companion play to *An Englishman Abroad*, *A Question of Attribution*, is also both an insider and an outsider. He is a well-known art historian, works at the prestigious Courtauld Institute, and is Keeper of the Queen's Pictures. Like Burgess and Hilary, he has betrayed England while remaining English, or, more exactly, is English in his betrayal. This irony is emphasized at the end when Blunt says to the secret service man, Chubb, that the 'great and the good' who were at the Academy Dinner were 'on [his] list', while the suburban investigator is ironically excluded from the occasion and admits he would 'feel a bit lost' at it. Unlike Burgess, however, Blunt is not a seducer; he is a 'cold fish'. It is interesting that in the stage production Bennett acted the patrician Blunt rather than Chubb, and this suggests a further analogy between this spy and the writer. From the initial stage image, through its structural transitions, jokes and play with parallels, *A Question of Attribution* constantly invites us to find analogies and multiple meanings, and consequently to interpret them. At the same time, a contradictory anxiety has been built into the play about the writer himself being exposed to the very interpretation he has invited.

The stage image at the beginning of the play is of Blunt and the Restorer: 'Their positions resemble those of saints or patrons on either side of an altarpiece and some effort should be made in the production to create stage pictures which echo in this way the composition and lighting of old masters.' Bennett wishes the production to suggest analogies between art and the life of the stage world as often as possible. He does not say what he wishes to imply by this. What is important is not how we interpret this stage effect, but the fact that analogy itself is emphasized and that the response it invites is first that we should laugh at the wit and then interpret its implications.

Analogies are built into the structure of the play, and the wit that invents them is one source of the pleasure that the comedy gives. The transitions between one episode and the next are managed in such a way that parallels and double meanings are suggested. Near the beginning, Blunt gives a lecture on Renaissance religious painting, in the course of which he reflects on martyrdom. Towards the end of the lecture, he says of paintings in which two episodes are simultaneously present, '. . . and did the saint but turn his head he would see his own martyrdom through the window'. At this point the stage directions instruct Blunt to turn, and the audience sees the door open and Chubb walk in. The similarity between the event and the painting suggests analogies between Blunt's situation and that of the martyr, a suggestion that is reinforced by his next word: 'Judas'. Then the slides of Renaissance paintings change to photographs of various young college men of the thirties, and the relationship is established between slides belonging to Chubb and Blunt as we move from the lecture to the interview between them. Later, as we watch a sequence of Chubb's slides, one of *Titian and a Venetian Senator* comes on to the screen, and a transition is made to Blunt in conversation with the Restorer and asking, 'But who is the new man?' (an image revealed when cleaning the picture). The slides of young men are resumed as Chubb returns.

The fact that the paintings and the photographs can replace one another so fluidly and naturally suggests that they are interchangeable. We are invited to interpret why this should be so. The comic climax of Part One comes as the slides mix again. Chubb is showing more of his photographs for identification when Blunt, after a monotonous series of 'No', says 'Actually that face does ring a bell' – but it is the face of Titian's son that he has recognized. This is the moment when Blunt, not Chubb, gets the clue about how to identify his unidentified man. Near the end of the play, Blunt gives his Academy lecture, tentatively identifying the figure revealed by the cleaning as Titian's son, and warning of the dangers of scholarship. At this point in the lecture, 'the light grows' on Chubb, who warns Blunt he will be exposed. Blunt uses exactly the same words to him as he did in his Academy lecture: 'Both our professions carry the same risks . . . a barrenness of outlook, a pedantry that verges on the obsessive, a farewell to commonsense, the rule of the hobby horse'.

A Question of Attribution is also full of puns and jokes that exploit the double meanings of language. A repeated pattern turns on the ambiguity of pronouns:

CHUBB: When she was visiting Surrey.
BLUNT: Your wife?
CHUBB: The Queen.

The character of HMQ produces multiple puns which turn on the comic fact that the same vocabulary can be attributed to paintings and the establishment world of MI5: '. . . a certain respectability . . . its background and pedigree are impeccable – besides, it has been vetted by the experts'. 'I was talking about art,' says Blunt after this. 'I'm not sure that she was.' He says 'I could have fallen flat on my face' reproachfully, only to find that metaphorically he has done just that. HMQ follows this up as she leaves, with 'One could have a nasty fall', and Blunt's student, Phillips, has the same sort of line when he says, 'There was a leak' (both of information and from a swimming pool). The wit comes from the fact that language functions literally and metaphorically at the same time, having the same kind of double meaning as the situation in the play.

The play constantly invites us to identify and interpret the relationships and multiple meanings it suggests. The central analogy is between Blunt investigating the newly discovered figure on the canvas, and Chubb investigating spies hidden in the Establishment. Burgess, Philby and Maclean all escaped to Russia, but there were rumours of a fourth and fifth man, one of whom turns out to be Blunt. He has a canvas on which there are now three figures, and in the final lecture he says that 'X-ray revealed a fourth man' and then a fifth. Chubb and Blunt are each trying to find the identities of their own types of hidden figures, using slides. Blunt suggests a tentative identification of his third figure. Chubb, also looking for the 'names behind the names', warns Blunt, with a verbal echo and a pun, 'You will be named. Attributed.'

'Attributed' points to a further analogy – between fakes. A fake is defined by HMQ as something that 'is not what it is claimed to be'. Blunt is investigating a painting which has been attributed to Titian and which is now thought not to be by him. HMQ thinks that her picture is therefore a fake, though Blunt denies this, saying it has only been wrongly attributed. Blunt himself is a fake by HMQ's definition. As a spy, he is not what he claims to be. HMQ lets him know this in the speech where her double meanings take in MI5 as well as the art world. Blunt says to her that the 'public are rather tiresomely fascinated by forgery – more so, I'm afraid, than they are by the real thing'. When he is about to be exposed, his words closely echo this, and the same analogy applies: 'as a fake' he too will 'excite more interest than the genuine article'.

A further theme which the pattern of analogies points to is the wish to get to the bottom of things, to find out what they are 'really like'. It motivates both of the investigators, Blunt and Chubb. Chubb tries to find out about more than spies. He (and his wife) are curious about the Queen: 'What is she really like?' he asks twice. It is ironic that Chubb is trying to coax Blunt into such gossip, which for a royal servant would be a breach of the Official Secrets Act. Chubb is also searching for a 'map' of history and concepts with which to find his way around the world of art, which to him is a mystery that he is determined to 'crack'. Blunt speaks in similar terms of the picture: it is a 'riddle' which he cannot claim to have solved. HMQ and Blunt also discuss portrait painters, who HMQ says are supposed to reveal, using the phrase once more, 'what one's really like'. This turns the artist into an investigator, as the detective and the art historian already are. All wish to uncover hidden meanings, to unmask what HMQ calls 'the secret self'. Blunt acknowledges these protected inner worlds: 'I think the only person who doesn't have a secret self, Ma'am, must be God . . . There is no sense in which one could ask, "What is God really like?".'

But though the play invites investigation and uncovers the investigators themselves, it also strongly resists the process. Resistance begins with the Official Secrets Act, which Blunt breached and which it is Chubb's business to protect. This Act is invoked to remind Blunt that 'keeping mum' is part of a royal servant's life. 'But of course you don't open your mouth', says another royal servant, Colin, to Phillips. HMQ is unwilling to have her secret self laid bare by portrait painters, ('I don't think one wants to be captured, does one?'; 'they get me wrong') though Blunt assures her that 'none of them quite capture you'. Blunt finds his position, with his secret self having been laid bare, to be a kind of martyrdom. People dislike and resist being unmasked. So do works of art, though we see Blunt working hard to unmask the mysteries of the painting. He warns Chubb that to understand an artist's meaning is not something which one can do 'automatically' or with a 'kit'. To do so would be to carry Chubb's techniques into an area where they would not be appropriate. An image may be allegorical, with one meaning; it may have multiple meanings; it may just be itself. Art is elusive: 'Art is seldom quite what it seems.' Blunt is twice given speeches in which he tries to protect art from reductive interpretation and claims that its meaning eludes investigation. The second speech is his climactic Academy Dinner lecture: 'paintings . . . are not there primarily to be solved. A great painting will still elude us, as art will always elude exposition'. In view of the multiple analogies in the play he is probably also warning Chubb that there is no kit for cracking the puzzle of a human self either. Blunt also admits the danger to the person who attempts to solve the puzzles of human beings or of art: 'a life spent teasing out riddles of this kind carries its own risks . . . a barrenness of outlook, a pedantry that verges on the obsessive'.

One could suggest that the playwright, an artist in another medium, is another investigator. *A Question of Attribution* is a work of art which draws attention to its own artfulness. Bennett investigates Blunt and he takes on Chubb's question about HMQ and what she is like to 'Hob-nob with. As a person'. His portraits (I use the word deliberately) of what HMQ and Blunt are 'really like' are only speculative, of course, but part of the play's attraction is that it appeals to the same curiosity that it examines critically: the wish to know about royalty and spies, and to get to their secret selves.

A further analogy might be that the playwright too has an active and hidden inner world which he is concerned to protect. There are two secret selves in a work of art: the implied meanings (which we have been warned will elude us), and the secret self of the artist, for the play is the product of his knowledge, his wit and his imagination (which we have been warned he will not want to have 'captured'). Playwrights are also artists whose meaning is sought. Like Blunt, they are both the investigators and the investigated. The writer is exposed to curiosity. He is vulnerable to the very people who are interested in him, and Bennett dislikes this: 'Authors resent the knowledge of themselves they have volunteered to their readers', he wrote in *The*

London Review of Books. He might well be glad of another Official Secrets Act.

Critics are among these investigators whom Bennett resents, as they also wish to uncover the secret self of the work. Like Chubb, they too risk barrenness and pedantry and seeing a work as a problem to be solved, a puzzle to 'crack'. Perhaps the best they can hope for is that their curiosity about it can be called speculative and playing with analogies, just as Bennett himself does in the play – though often not, alas, with Bennett's elegance, inventiveness and wit!

10   The Writer Out of Disguise

Two Kafka Plays

In addition to the plays which offer oblique suggestions about the writer's experience, Bennett has written two plays which are overtly about one particular writer: Kafka. *The Insurance Man* is the first, filmed in the summer of 1985 and shown on television in February 1986. The second, *Kafka's Dick*, was first performed in the Royal Court Theatre in September 1986. Given how strongly Bennett in *A Question of Attribution* objects to talking about artists, it is interesting to see how he writes about a major author.

Bennett celebrates Kafka, and he does so in two quite different dramatic modes. Each play has a different emphasis on the 'fun' and 'pain' which he identifies in his introduction, and which his own tragicomic talent values in Kafka. Both plays are soaked in paradox and contradiction, which emerge in the television film as dark and ironic, and in the stage play as fantastic and exuberantly verbal comedy.

The Insurance Man

In *The Insurance Man*, Bennett celebrates Kafka by demonstrating how close Kafka's work is to reality: he uses some of Kafka's strategies to suggest that his nightmares are ways of seeing the real world and psychologically exact. But, even so, he does not absolve Kafka from his share of writer's guilt, and the play leaves the viewer with an uncomfortable suggestion of the disjunction between the public figure and the private man.

Of course, we assume the insurance man is Kafka, since he must be the most famous one ever. He appears in the play as an employee of the Workers' Accident Insurance Institute (WAII) in 1910, but he is not the central figure in the story. That distinction belongs to Franz, a young employee in a dyeworks. The first part of the film briskly progresses through the sequence of events that brings Franz to the WAII: he develops a skin disease as a result of his job; he shows it to a doctor but hides it from his fiancée; he is dismissed from his job; a girl in the firm's office tells him that he is insured and should seek compensation; he then arrives at the WAII.

At this point, the camera leaves Franz to show the institute at work: it travels through a series of offices where claimants are being interviewed, and ends in Kafka's, where he is telling his secretary that his brother-in-law is starting a factory. Then the film returns to Franz, and he is plunged into the crazy and frustrating world of the Institute. He is sent to Kafka, but they manage to miss each other narrowly four times, frustrating his hopes and his quest by this farcically repeated pattern. He wanders around the building, allowing both him and the audience to glimpse vignettes of WAII heartlessness. His frustration breaks out in violence to Lily, a crazed claimant who undertakes to help him. He finally sees a doctor and is exposed naked to an audience of medical students. Meanwhile, at a presentation ceremony for their Head of Department, Kafka makes a speech about the Institute. His witty account of its illogic and his warnings about its 'hardness of heart' are intercut with the desperate Franz trying to get to see him.

Finally, as the play moves to its climax, the two of them meet. Franz accuses Kafka of being worse than his colleagues, since he understands the pain of Franz's experience but does nothing to prevent it. Kafka offers Franz a job in his brother-in-law's new factory. There are then two shots of Kafka working and coughing in the factory, which sandwich a scene in which Franz's fiancée breaks up with him. In the second of these scenes, Franz arrives to thank Kafka: his skin has cleared, and he will take the job. He has a new fiancée, the girl from the office who told him to make an insurance claim. It is a happy ending, and Franz tells Kafka that he 'has saved his life'. But the last lines reveal for the first time that this is an asbestos factory and that the coughing is caused by asbestos dust.

However, there is another aspect to the film's structure. The story is actually told as a flashback, and it is framed at the beginning and end by other events. It opens in Prague in 1945 while the Russians are liberating the city, with a corpse hanging in the street outside a doctor's surgery. Franz comes to the doctor, as an old man, to hear the result of lung X-rays. The film closes by returning to the surgery. Franz is told he is going to die of lung cancer, possibly caused by asbestos. As the doctor shows him out, the corpse is still hanging there, and the doctor says that the victim had come for refuge to the house next door, had been admitted into what he thought was safety and had found his pursuers were there before him. The film ends with a silhouette of the corpse showing through the glass of the closed door.

This is a curious way to make a film about Kafka. First, he is made into an important but secondary character; second, there is not a single mention of his being a writer. What we see is only his ordinary everyday job, his public business life. He is often seen from the outside: we hear comments from his colleagues. He is treated with respect, known to have a degree, to work hard, to be Jewish. We are told he is 'calm' and we see he is tactful among his colleagues. Kafka's linguistic gifts and intellectual power are recognized. He is known to be a fluent speaker and asked to make a speech at an office ceremony, which he does competently and amusingly; he is known to be interested in 'borderline case[s]'. This last phrase implies the detachment that his job involves: it is his business as an insurance man to assess the disastrous experiences of others. (Whose did he assess as a writer?) With one exception, he is referred to throughout the play by his second name, Kafka, the name which his readers also use.

Franz, on the other hand, is the character whose private anxieties and suffering we are shown and with whom we are asked to empathize, and he is known throughout the film only by his first name, which was also Kafka's. The coincidence of the name suggests that the two characters are in some way doubles, opposite halves of a shared identity. The title too makes them share an identity: Kafka is the insurance man because he works in insurance; Franz, because he is trying to make an insurance claim. They are linked by being opposites, as they are shown to be by Kafka's first appearance in the film. He is admitted into the WAII with respect and through the main door by the same doorman who rudely holds back Franz and directs him to a side door. Much of the film is about these two opposites trying to find each other, and their meeting is its climax.

The doubling also suggests a split in Bennett's own mind. Kafka's role in the film implies that the writer is a person who has to function in the world just like anyone else. He also demonstrates the writer as he is perceived publicly: the man who is interested in borderline cases and has an unusual ability to verbalize his perceptions. Franz implies the writer's private self, experiencing the pains of life, the tension of being a borderline case. In that sense, he represents the raw material of experience to which the writer gives public form. That experience includes the desire to make sense of his private bewilderment by giving utterance to it publicly: 'I want it to be given a name. How can I ever get rid of it if it doesn't have a name?' Franz says of his skin complaint. When the two opposites do meet, the experience is uncomfortable, and Franz accuses Kafka of the same writer's guilt that Bennett ascribes to himself in the preface to *Two Kafka Plays*. Kafka tries to help and Franz is grateful, but their lives stay separate and Franz is ultimately destroyed by Kafka's good intentions. Between the public and private self of the writer there is never ease or unity.

If Franz in some way suggests the subjective experience and vision which are the raw materials of the writer, it is not surprising that the suffering of Bennett's Franz has much in common with what Kafka exposes his characters to. The way he is made to see the world by Bennett's dramatic strategies shares the strange blend of nightmare and reality that Kafka's characters live in. As Bennett does these things, he celebrates Kafka's achievement by emphasizing both his technical experiments and his truth.

Bennett creates Franz's experience of Kafka in the WAII by using visual images that echo Kafka's own strategies as a writer. Because he manages to blend Kafka's dreamlike distortions stylistically with the conventions of dramatic realism, he can suggest how much of Kafka's imaginary world is a way of seeing the everyday one. The opening shot of a corpse hanging in a street suggests the dark mood of the play, though the claustrophobic interior shots begin only when Franz enters the WAII. It is then that the play moves – Kafka-like – to what Bennett calls 'the frontiers of dreams'. Bennett's instructions to camera and director are explicit about this: 'The topography of the offices in general is intricate and illogical ... like the topography of a dream'; '... small sliding panels ... another odd dream-like feature'. He mentions several ways in which the film could suggest the distortions which make the WAII appear nightmarish: 'The shot should emphasize the machinery of the gates'; Franz, lost, runs up a winding staircase littered with papers – he 'climbs a poky staircase, which we see from above as if it is a vortex'; the inquiries window 'should go up and down like a rat-trap. Any odd *Alice in Wonderland* features like this should be emphasized'. Later, a group waiting outside the Tribunal 'should be reminiscent of characters in *Alice in Wonderland*'. The group forms a row of grotesques who turn Franz into an object of scrutiny, just as the Mad Hatter's tea party did to Alice. What *Alice in Wonderland* means to Bennett is made clear in the introduction, where Carroll is associated with Dickens and Kafka as writers whose topography is 'burrows and garrets and cubby holes on back staircases'. Dickens, like Kafka, uses his dream landscapes to attack institutions as an enemy of the individual. All the writers create a landscape which suggests the strangeness of secret interiors, and the frustrations and anxiety of clarity denied, just like the nightmarish, threatening place Bennett has created for Franz and the other claimants.

Nightmarish it may be, but the place is not a surreal one: it is firmly rooted in reality. The opening sets the play in the historical nightmare of Prague in 1945. There is nothing fantastic about the corpse, any more than there is about the doctor's surgery, the X-rays or the questions about the patient's history. The people waiting outside the Tribunal who look like characters out of *Alice in Wonderland* are grotesque and simplified, but their grotesqueness has roots in painful reality: they lack ears, limbs and hair as a result of industrial accidents.

Though the dialogue abounds in wit and tragi-comic paradoxes ('Accidents, as we well know, are never an accident'; 'Previously an optimist she is now a pessimist, is that such a bad thing?'), there is plenty of evidence of Bennett's ear for inconsequential ordinary speech. When Franz's landlady brings him tea, she sounds like a character from one of Bennett's plays of contemporary Leeds: 'You can't show me anything new. My husband was in the armed forces . . . This room used to be let to a fully fledged optician . . . He had diplomas'. So does the old man in the factory: 'Funny process, dyeing. Saw a lad once, scales from there down . . . That were t'dye.' The play remains within the conventions of realism, and none of the events is fantastic. It was shot on location in Liverpool and Bradford. When Bennett felt the designers had overdone the dust for a scene in a disused Bradford factory, it turned out that they had touched nothing at all. Film shot like this is a medium that lends itself to realism and Bennett's television plays are mainly realist, but it also lends itself to photographing the real world so that we see it in distorted ways. Bennett's dramatic style indicates how much Kafka's work is a way of seeing the ordinary world. We are asked to see the WAII as 'a terrible place' and, as Bennett says of Kafka's own topography, as a 'shorthand for desolation'.

In the film, Bennett recognizes the truth of Kafka's account of desolation: the ironies, contradictions and anxieties of everyday life. He recognizes the same contradictions and desolation in the world outside fiction. In his introductions to the two Kafka plays, he tells of his own visit to a hospital and concludes that, exactly as in the WAII, 'permanent staff resent those for whose benefit the institution exists'. He notices the graffiti on a bus stop in Liverpool: 'Hope is fucking hopeless' and the contradictions between the mosaics on the floor of St George's Hall ('He hath given me skill that He might be honoured') and the stickers on the wall saying 'Save the pits'.

It is only a small step from this to the paradoxes which Franz experiences in the WAII. The paradox at the heart of Kafka's short story, 'The Burrow' ('His refuge turns out to be his doom'), is also at the heart of the film: the 1945 episode framing the main narrative shows the doom, while the 1910 events show Franz's frustration and the apparent refuge he is offered. Caught in a world 'where loss determines gain . . . and to limp is to jump every hurdle', Franz hungers for explanations and clarity, but he does not get them. He is doomed, like Joseph K in *The Trial*, to live with frustration and uncertainty. Lily, the crazed claimant, is on the same hopeless quest. She needs to see the Institution as comprehensible and positive, and tries to make Franz join in her deluded way of seeing. In one of the darkest moments of the play, Franz is driven by her obstinate denial of what is under her nose – that the institution does not recognize her existence, and that she does not know her way around it – and also by his own frustration into making a violent attack on her.

The world represented by Bennett's Kafka-like institution makes no response to Franz's fear and desire. Bennett says specifically that one of his jokes was to 'emphasize the heartlessness of the officials and the desperation of the injured workpeople'. Again and again, he makes the staff unfeeling: 'Dustbin job', says one, passing Franz's papers on to somewhere else in the system. 'Out. Out. Out', screams a clerk at claimants; a girl stands naked before a tribunal of doctors; Franz himself is stripped and lectured on. When Kafka warns colleagues against the hazards of their job, he speaks of 'blindness to genuine need . . . and hardness of heart', against which there are no safety precautions. But the play is more ambivalent than a simple split between needy claimants and heartless Institute, or indeed a pathetic man in an unresponsive world. Bennett, like Kafka, begins to turn his character's quest for compensation into something psychologically deeper. The Angry Doctor, in his one scene, voices the problem. We feel that it is normal to be perfect and happy, and that life owes us something if it turns out to be less than that. There is a blurred dividing line between genuine accidents for which compensation might be claimed, and the changes and chances of this mortal life, which we can also feel to be unjust. The Angry Doctor points out that we have no claim against life in the name of justice: 'We cannot compensate people for being cast out of Paradise.' Lily is the mad result of a belief that they can and do. Insurance, Kafka's public business, is turned into an ironic symbol. This point is made explicit as the play nears its end, when Kafka's secretary says, 'People will be wanting compensation for being alive next.' The stage instructions tell Kafka to look 'as if this might not be a bad idea'.

If, like Kafka's heroes, Franz is doomed to uncertainty and frustration, like them, he is also doomed to the certainty of mortality. The film makes yet another use of the doubling of the characters, when Bennett makes Franz live an alternative life that Kafka himself might have led. He points out how Kafka's own death was Kafka-like in its irony. His doom turned out in a way to be his refuge, for, as Bennett writes in the introduction, if he had not died of TB in 1924 he would probably have died in the Holocaust as did his sisters, and if he had somehow avoided that he might have died of lung cancer induced by asbestos – 'Death took no chances with Kafka'. What interests Bennett seems to be the relief we feel when we manage to 'escape' from death. But of course we do not escape: we can only postpone. Fleeing from anxiety and death is another hopeless quest, and any refuge we find will eventually turn out to contain our doom. Bennett was not able to dramatize this irony by telling Kafka's own story, since he did not escape from TB, his first mortal danger. Instead, Bennett invents a character to whom he gives Kafka's first name, and makes him survive, if not the Holocaust (Franz is not said to be a Jew), then at least the Nazi occupation of Prague, only to die from lung cancer caused by his earlier exposure to asbestos. The play places the 'happy' story of 1910 between the two 1945 scenes in which Franz receives his death sentence. The opening and closing shots of the corpse symbolize the ironic paradox at the heart of the play. In this context, we recognize the irony of Franz's early line, 'So I'm not going to die.' Nobody can ever say that. Kafka and his fictional counterpart, Franz, live opposite life patterns, but meet the same end, as does everyone.

Finally, Bennett uses Kafka to reflect on the writer's situation: his guilty collusion with a world whose pain he can articulate more clearly than most. Bennett quotes a dark insight from Kafka: 'to write is to do the devil's work'. Kafka, who attacks institutions so vehemently, himself works for the Institute, and is so much part of it that he finds it 'almost cosy'. The writer can easily become part of the establishment whose shortcomings he attacks in his work. In the introduction, Bennett confesses to feeling writer's guilt when making the film in Liverpool. Faced with the run-down city, he found that producing a play 'seems tactless where there is no work'. He had felt the same when filming *Me, I'm Afraid of Virginia Woolf* in a 'desperate' part of Leeds: 'the line insults them. I insult them'. He identifies himself with a person who is in the best position to know and yet does nothing: 'One glibly despises the photographer who zooms in on the starving child ... without offering help. Writing is not different.'

Bennett makes his Kafka share this guilt, and the climax of the play is organized to make this point. When the questing individual finally meets the writer, the best hope of clarity and humanity that he could find in the Institute, Franz hopes to find another 'human being'. Kafka will admit only to being 'a very good imitation' of one. He asks Franz, 'What did you want to say to me?', but from this point, Franz is given only two sentences in almost two pages of dialogue: 'You are harder to see than anybody' and 'I don't want money'. Having, like Joseph K, finally reached the person to whom he looks for a verdict, Franz has no demand to make. On the other hand, the writer Kafka talks. He echoes the Angry Doctor's insight when he says, 'You are asking for a justice that doesn't exist in the world.' He tells Franz that his story and condition are brought about by 'many small accidents that we cannot see or record'. He says, 'I do understand' – and indeed he does. Then comes Franz's challenge: 'if you understand and you don't help, you're wicked, you're evil'. 'This is a terrible place', he says, and it is a judgement on Kafka that he should find it 'almost cosy'. As they part, Kafka tries to help: he offers Franz a job in his brother-in-law's factory. But, as Franz leaves, Kafka, with a gesture which suggests washing his hands of him, removes the last traces of his visitor – 'some small bits of skin that have adhered to his hand'. After this come the two short scenes in the factory and the 'happy ending', but the last word of this happy ending is the ominous word 'asbestos', held back until now. Kafka's help will lead to Franz's eventual death, as the final scene of the film shows. The writer ends compromised. Bennett and Kafka share the writer's guilt at being part of the system, and if their writing shows how well they understand the system, then ironically they are all the more guilty. By putting Franz at the centre and not Kafka, the writer can be presented not simply as passive, as in *The Writer in Disguise*, but from the point of view of the disadvantaged for whom his power and understanding change nothing. In this, *The Insurance Man* resembles *Enjoy*, although the guilt has a different emphasis.

Bennett celebrates the achievements of Kafka by using similar strategies and exploring how real and immediate are the ironies and anxieties which Kafka responded to in his world. But he sees him as uncomfortably divided, and in that divide grows the moral guilt that Bennett seems to think the inevitable part of any writer's vocation.

Kafka's Dick

The second play, *Kafka's Dick*, is an outlandish and farcical comedy. In it, Bennett pays tribute to how accurately Kafka's fantasies reflect the real world; he draws attention to a neglected quality in Kafka's work – humour ('*The Trial* . . . is a funnier book than it has got credit for'). Bennett once again explores the writer's situation, by focusing on why Kafka should have wished his work to be destroyed after his death. This play brings Kafka back to life into our contemporary world, only to find himself a cultural monument, the subject of a critical and bio-graphical industry; his private life is laid open for public consumption; and his work, as Auden puts it in his elegy on Yeats, has been 'modified in the guts of the living'.

The structure of *Kafka's Dick* is very simple. It starts with Kafka's death-bed request to Brod, his friend and future biographer, to destroy his work. Kafka offers no explanation for this: the play itself gives the audience his reasons. However, he does display a comical ambivalence about the annihilation. When Brod promptly and obediently moves to go out and buy some paraffin, Kafka stops him and begins to make difficulties, and 'brighten[s]' when Brod shows signs of demurring. Brod has almost managed to persuade Kafka to change his mind when he mistakenly refers to Gregor Samsa, the character who turns into a beetle in Kafka's *Metamorphosis*, as a 'cockroach'. This slip makes up Kafka's mind for him: 'You write one thing, the reader makes it into another,' he says. 'Burn them.' And he says there is to be no biography though, as Brod points out, if there is no work, there will be no need for biography, so his ambivalence remains evident.

Then the play shifts forward in time to the present, to a house occu-pied by Sydney, Linda, his wife, and his father. Sydney works in insur-ance, as Kafka did, is an expert on Kafka and has published an article on him. Sydney's father is waiting unwillingly to be inspected by a social worker and possibly taken into a home. Kafka's dick is intro-duced here: Sydney explains that two psychologists have deduced the small size of his penis from his work and published their conclusions. Once this household has been established, Bennett brings into it, one after the other, Brod, Kafka, Hermann (Kafka's father) and Julie (his mother).

This fantastic plot is comically introduced. Brod, having an elderly bladder, rings Sydney's doorbell to ask to use their lavatory, but he has waited too long and urinates on their tortoise instead. The scene with Brod establishes that Linda is more interesting to Brod than Sydney is, and also sets up the antagonism between the two experts on Kafka. Further, it introduces the theme of fame: the famous people in the past are still alive; others are dead.

Linda goes to the kitchen to wash her tortoise, and we hear her scream off stage. There has been another kind of metamorphosis: the tortoise has changed into Kafka. Like Brod, he is more interested in Linda than Sydney. Brod realizes that Kafka, who is now in a house full of books by and about himself, will soon discover that his dying request was ignored, and he fears that the writer will reject him. He and Sydney embark on an attempt to avoid embarrassment and exposure that is straight out of farce: it begins with their realization that Kafka will discover the truth ('Weidenfeld and Nicolson! His books!') and continues with much rushing around concealing evidence. They have to improvise explanations to Kafka ('Pornography . . . (Sydney looks hurt.)') until finally, to their horror, Kafka picks up a book. The audience waits for the explosion – and it turns out anti-climactically to be a novel by Proust. Finally, the doddering father brings a paperback of *The Trial* back into the room, disappointed that it is not a detective story. As the first half of the play nears its end, the truth comes out. Kafka learns that he 'speak[s] mankind's farewell in the authentic voice of the twentieth century' (to which his response is 'Shit') and that he is now 'a vast building; a ramshackle institution' (which sounds very like an establishment that Kafka himself would invent). The doorbell rings and a policeman enters. He turns out to be Hermann Kafka, and the act ends with 'Hello, my son'.

Hermann is contemptuous of his son as a man, and indifferent to him as a writer. However, he becomes interested when Sydney, piqued by Kafka's dislike of his ardent fans and his obvious attraction to Linda, says that Franz Kafka is worse than the books present him as being. Having learnt of his own notoriety, Hermann sees an opportunity to rewrite history by presenting himself as less appalling and his son as less admirable than the usual version of their lives makes them. He tempts Sydney to write a biography of Kafka using this revised picture, promising him fame for revolutionizing academic study of his son. He then blackmails Kafka into agreeing that he lied about his father by threatening to reveal that Kafka's penis is very small. There is a comic scene full of *double entendres* as Kafka caves in. Brod tries to justify the usual version of Kafka and Hermann by referring to Kafka's famous letter to his father, and the section ends with Hermann reading it.

The social worker now arrives, and she also undergoes a metamorphosis: this time into Julie Kafka. Kafka is put on trial for having taken Brod and Hermann's names from them by his fame. Linda thinks that the men are protesting about conditions that women have always been expected to put up with. Kafka outlines the sort of society in which he would be willing to be read, and then Sydney's father reappears. As soon as he says, 'I'm a normal parent. Nobody remembers me', Hermann realizes that his new image will not bring him fame. He is 'in the text' only because he was a bad father. His attempted blackmail emerges, but it causes hardly a ripple of interest. (Everybody on stage knew about Kafka's dick anyway: it was already in a book.) There is a speech about the myth of an artist's life, and the play ends, rather unsatisfactorily, with a party given by Hermann as God ('I'm the Host') in a Heaven in which there is no literature.

This play, like *The Insurance Man*, honours Kafka by finding ways to dramatize how accurately Kafka's apparent fantasies reflect the real world and also finds a theatrical style which combines reality and fantasy. In the stage directions Bennett writes, 'I am not sure how representational the room should be.' It needs to be representational enough to give the message that Linda, Sydney and Father are an ordinary suburban family: Kafka's vision and legacy are examined in that context. But extraordinary things happen and the metamorphosis of the tortoise parodies Kafka's most famous invention.

It is the imperceptive Sydney who says to Linda, 'You wouldn't like his stories. Not what you'd call "true to life"', an opinion which the play denies. Sydney's father is introduced as 'an old man with a Zimmer frame'. It is a real – and sad – situation: the old man, physically incapacitated, fearing that his mind is going, is waiting for the verdict of the social worker and to be sentenced to the old people's home. The metaphors 'verdict' and 'sentence' are so ordinary that they are almost dead, but they are the ones on which Kafka based *The Trial*. That the very ordinary situation of Sydney's father can be presented in Kafka's terms implies how much Kafka writes about commonplaces. There are even verbal echoes: 'Someone's been telling lies about me,' says Father, twice, echoing the opening sentence of *The Trial*. 'They've come to take me away and I don't know what I've done,' he says, summarizing its plot, including its fear of the anonymous and authoritative 'them'. A running joke in the play is that Sydney's father is preparing to answer questions in order to prove his mental capacity. He is asked if he has heard of Kafka ('if you're supposed to know the name of Czech novelists everybody's going to end up in a home') and later if he has heard of Kafka's father ('The buggers! Every time you're ready for the examination, they change the syllabus,' he says, outlining a plot which Kafka might well have invented). To protect himself, he learns to parrot the received wisdom that Hermann was 'Dreadful. And a shocking bully', only to be contradicted by Hermann himself. This type of running joke belongs to farce. It also grimly indicates the frustrations of the old man's attempt to prove his sanity. He is perfectly lucid, but dramatically peripheral to the twists and turns of the action. As a result, he does not know why he is being asked these questions or why he is told that his answers are wrong. 'I never imagine things,' he says, and it is true. But as he says it his eye falls on Brod's hat moving slowly across the floor. We know the reason: Brod has put his hat down on the tortoise. But the father thinks that he is going crazy, and bolts. We are more likely to allow the father's story symbolic overtones because he parallels both Hermann, the other father on trial in the play, and Kafka himself, who is literally put on trial, with the old man's Zimmer frame acting as the dock. This is farce used to dramatize real anxieties, and so the sub-plot roots Kafka's fiction in the tragi-comic commonplaces of life.

Bennett gives an unusual emphasis to Kafka's humour, especially the way it combines 'fun' and 'pain', a gift which they share. It was a joke made by Kafka on his sickbed that started Bennett writing about him, quite literally a sick joke ('I think I deserve the Nobel Prize for sputum') and Bennett observes that 'Kafka's jokes about himself are better for the desperate circumstances in which they were often made', mixing fun and pain in his actual life.

There is an interesting example of how Bennett's tragi-comic mix illuminates Kafka's in the introduction to *Two Kafka Plays*. Trying to illustrate how someone might say of *The Trial* 'But that's my story!' Bennett writes a short story himself. Mr Jay (not K) is in hospital for investigation. We recognize he has cancer; he does not. He is given *The Trial* as a mystery story by the ward's library lady. He is disappointed and can make little of such sentences as 'The verdict doesn't come all at once; the proceedings gradually merge into the verdict'. Of course, that is Mr Jay's story too, and if he had read on he might have recognized that Kafka could have been talking about him.

It is a painful story, but the narrator's voice is comic, even skittish. There are jokes: hospital reading and hospital food both are 'lacking taste' and neither has 'much in the way of roughage'. The library lady, because she is single and 'has no figure to speak of . . . is generally taken to be rather refined and thus has got landed with literature'. She is a simple comic stereotype, but the fun merges with pain in Bennett's comment that 'The real life sentences come from judgements on our personal appearance and good behaviour, far from remitting the sentence, simply . . . makes it lifelong'. The experience of Mr Jay and the woman is from Kafka's world and once more the metaphor used of its cruel and comic paradox is that of a trial. The comic imagination and paradoxical wit with which Bennett tells the story is a critical tribute to Kafka.

Kafka's Dick opens with laughter in the face of death, caused by an extreme example of the contradictory desires driving most of the characters. Brod receives Kafka's request to destroy his books: 'He says he's dying then suddenly it's "if". Don't you mean "when"?' Bennett's dying Kafka is an absurd figure because he is illogical, wanting to have it both ways. He wants his work destroyed and preserved. Later, he is 'happily lugubrious'; he has 'a name for anonymity'. Linda sees him clearly when she says, 'Enjoy yourself. Be miserable.' Other characters are contradictory too. 'Fame is a continuing offence,' says Sydney, who would also like to be famous. Julie and Hermann have the following dialogue:

JULIE: You didn't like our son?
HERMANN: No.
JULIE: But then you said you did.
HERMANN: Yes.
JULIE: And now you say you didn't.
HERMANN: Yes.

To this, Julie's reply is 'Is that what they mean by Kafkaesque?' Here, the description is applied to the ambivalence of human desire. The contradiction is absurd, and so is expressed in the paradoxical jokes which are the characteristic wit of this play, but the desire is endlessly unsatisfied and therefore painful. To Bennett, Kafka's desperate laughter is at the same time fantastic, and true of the ordinary world.

However, the main ambivalence on which the play focuses is Kafka's: he is in two minds about being famous, about being known, and about being read. This is a famous example of the artist's reluctance to be investigated, which Bennett wrote about more obliquely in another of his comedies, *A Question of Attribution*, a play with which *Kafka's Dick* has much in common. 'I don't want to be known,' Kafka tells Sydney, who is in the middle of writing an article on him. His wish for privacy gives rise to the passage of classic farce, when Sydney and Brod struggle to conceal from him that his novels have been published.

The curious title also emphasizes privacy, since it refers to what are still called private parts. There is a common taboo on exposure of the genitals, and in the introduction to *The Insurance Man*, Bennett admits that it is something from which his imagination shrinks. In that play, it is part of his presentation of dehumanizing bureaucracy when a young man and woman are exposed nude. Kafka's father blackmails him with exposure (another dead metaphor is brought to life), producing a great many puns as he does so: 'The long and the short of the matter is . . .'; 'There is one fact about my son and his. . . old man that has never got into print'. Kafka crumples under the threat and stays cowed until his father changes his mind – at which point both men discover that 'your private parts have long been public property', a characteristically para-doxical way of saying that his worst fears have come true. The critic and biographer are the people who threaten the writer with this dread-ed exposure, because they want to uncover the most private parts of their subject. They make his relationship with his parents, even his dreams, into public property. Sydney, the would-be critic, would like biographies to carry nude photographs. Two of the sharpest lines in the play are:

LINDA: Sydney. This is persecution.
SYDNEY: No, it's not. It's biography.

To use the metaphor again, Kafka fears that fame 'leaves you open to trial at any time'.

Further, he fears being misunderstood. Another running joke in the play is that Kafka wrote of Gregor Samsa turning into a beetle and that Brod and Sydney, in spite of his protests, persistently say 'cockroach'. Kafka complains that 'Nobody ever believed what I said about myself', though characteristically this speech ends in a tangle of paradoxes which suggest that understanding him would not be easy: 'Only now when at last you find I was telling the truth about myself you call me a liar.' He rejects everyone who might claim to understand him: fans, critics and biographers. When Sydney protests 'I've read your books . . . I'm a *fan*', Kafka turns from him to the unliterary Linda, who sees him the most clearly. That Bennett identifies with this is implied in the way he mocks literary critics by parodying their excessive ingenuity and mocking their possessiveness about their subject: '*Kafka* thinks he knows about Kafka. I'm the only one who really knows', says Brod.

But there is a contradictory desire for fame, which is coarsely present in Brod, Sydney and Hermann, who, comically, wants to be known as rotten. Fame is a defence against the fear of extinction: 'I'm famous. I exist,' says Kafka, making the two synonymous. Brod makes the same equation: 'I'm also famous. These are the dead ones. Nobody's ever heard of them. That's death. You read my book?' Sydney hopes that fame will follow if he writes the book overturning received ideas about Kafka. To be written about also brings fame: 'I'm a bad father, so I'm in the text,' proclaims Hermann. He chooses to be loathed and famous rather than be liked and forgotten. Brod, though he resents it, knows, 'If I hadn't been Kafka's friend I wouldn't have been in the play.' The existence of *Kafka's Dick* itself is confirmation that fame continues to confer life and that bad fathers are not forgotten.

Hermann cheerfully chooses fame at any cost. However, in Kafka, the conflict is unresolved. His ambivalence is the source of the comedy of the opening death-bed scene. His desire for publication is not stated overtly; it is a comic sub-text made explicit in the stage directions. Kafka brightens and 'clutch[es] at a straw' when Brod hesitates. He becomes gloomy when Brod lists the writers burnt by the Nazis in 1933 ('Don't I figure?' he asks). 'But I am nobody', he announces, making a big deal of humility. Linda's reply, 'Why *tell* us? Women can be nobodies all the time and who cares', is a sharp challenge to the good faith of such publicized modesty, and a reminder that there are areas which have to remain silent to be truthful.

This feminist criticism is unexpected, but is developed in a way that suggests the conflict about fame is more masculine than feminine. Neither of the female characters desires it, and the men assume their insignificance. 'You don't even make his subconscious', Hermann says to Julie; 'You'll be the wife of a famous man', Sydney assures Linda, who feels that this is treating her as the 'tree against which [he] cocked [his] leg'; the men argue about losing their names; Julie points out that women take this for granted when they marry.

The writer, for Bennett, is further split between being a man and a cultural monument. One of the strangest paradoxes in the play is 'He knows he's Kafka. He doesn't know he's *Kafka*.' Kafka denies being a literary icon:

SYDNEY: But you are Kafka.
KAFKA: No, I'm not. Kafka is . . . a ramshackle institution . . .'

Kafka wants to be a man, and he and Brod turn to the attractive Linda rather than to Sydney, with whom they share interests in writing and fame. Linda dramatizes the distinction between the man and the monument, by finding him 'nice' without having read a word of his books, and in another farcical moment is found by her husband in Kafka's arms. Yet his vanity also wants him to be more than just an ordinary man, and by seeing him as one, she undermines his self-dramatizing sense of his own specialness. 'But you'd agree I was a terrible human being?' he asks. 'No,' she says. 'Pretty average, if you ask me.' In paradoxes which meet him on his own ground, she puts her finger on the central contradiction in his being: '. . . like all men you believe your despair is important. You think you're insignificant but your insignificance is not insignificant.' Kafka claims this interesting pain as his own because he is a writer. Linda denies it to him: 'No. It's because you are a man.'

If biographers and critics desire fame like the writer, they also experience a writer's ambivalence. At the end of the play, Sydney echoes Kafka when he asks Linda to burn his manuscript, and she echoes Brod by obeying immediately. Bennett's Kafka fears that he may be exposed, misunderstood and possessed by critics. He also fears their ambivalence towards the writer as an admired authority, a parent figure ('. . . like the best and worst of fathers you have been an example and a reproach to writers ever since'). Brod and Hermann accuse Kafka of taking away their names, as they are known only in relation to him, though Brod was a prolific novelist himself. Their vanity is wounded by his fame. Like Sydney, they want to 'cut him down to size', which is why Sydney wants nude photographs in biographies and would rather 'read about writers than read what they write'.

Bennett finds a farcical and witty form for the absurdity of conflicting desires, exposing them in the particular form in which a writer experiences them, and there is no resolution. The revue turn with which the play ends finds Kafka in Heaven, but it is a heaven where God is played by his father and there is no literature. This resolves the conflict by taking away half the problem – but even that does not satisfy Kafka, ambivalent to the last. His final words are 'Heaven is going to be hell'.

Bennett's play is about a writer's conflict: his desire for privacy and his desire for fame. There is no resolution of this. It clearly puts the case for not writing about writers and not having a cultural industry. However, Bennett suggests that these conditions would be met only in a totalitarian state. Kafka, asked where he would be happiest, describes people reading his work in secret under Communist oppression, a strange irony in a writer who is famous for anticipating the experiences of men in a totalitarian bureaucracy.

This is Bennett's version of Kafka's dilemma as a writer: desire to be read and yet not to be known by his readers, and this is at the heart of the play. There is a further twist, as Bennett is also caught in the paradoxes that the play explores. Desiring not to be invaded or written on, he himself is writing about Kafka not wanting to be invaded or written about. It is no wonder that the dizzying perspectives of paradox, not logic, are central to the comic style of the play. ('If he did understand me he'd understand that I don't want to be understood,' complains Kafka). Here is the inconsistent spectacle of Bennett adding even more to the mass of commentary and speculation which surrounds Kafka. Like Sydney and Brod, he appropriates Kafka for his own ends: certainly to celebrate, but also to explore a situation important to himself.

Of course, when Bennett appropriates Kafka, he produces Bennett's version of Kafka (beetle or cockroach?). He feels affinities with the other writer: Kafka's 'fun and pain', irony, self-deprecation and paradoxes are all qualities of Bennett's writing too. Bennett admires these qualities in Kafka, and uses them himself to celebrate Kafka, but he knows that Kafka is put at risk by those very same qualities. Their shared gift of irony means that Bennett risks 'jok[ing] him down to size', much as the envious Sydney might try to do if only he had a sense of humour. Bennett has identified irony as a characteristic English trait as early as *The Old Country*, and knows that the way this trait manifests in himself may well produce an English version of Kafka: 'The Channel is a slipper bath of irony through which we pass these serious continentals in order not to be infected by their gloom. This propensity I am sure I have not escaped or tried to; but then there is something that *is* English about Kafka . . .'. Even the very sentence in which he states the problem is such an irony.

Logically, Bennett ought not to be writing the play at all. Why should this be an acceptable way to write about a writer? Perhaps, because he does it as a creative artist rather than as a critic, Bennett is exposing himself to the same risks that his Kafka fears – primarily, the risk of rejection. (Hermann voices the common human feeling, 'I wanted to be liked.') He might fail to be produced; he might not attract an audience and might fail to amuse them. Bennett exposes himself to possible criticism for self-contradiction, and also to the failure of his intellectual farce, one of the most risky things to write. Farce is one of the hardest forms to keep sparkling through a full-length work. How many English farces have lasted but *The Importance of Being Earnest*?

It is easy to imagine a play about Kafka in the style of documentary realism, which highlighted the same issues of the desire for privacy and the desire for fame by examining Kafka's sensitivity, his family relationships and his perfectionism, ending with his death. Realism, in a sense, ignores the presence of the writer, offering the illusion of seeing through the dramatic medium to the real person within. Realistic plays characteristically offer the illusion of watching an independent mind at work. *Hedda Gabler* purports to be an investigation of Hedda Gabler, but *The Importance of Being Earnest* foregrounds and therefore exposes the writer, as does *Kafka's Dick*. The audience is constantly aware that the pleasure which the play offers comes from what only the writer can invent: the pattern, the plotting, the mass of inter-relationships, and above all the verbal style, to which all the characters contribute, be they clever or stupid. Bennett, as a writer of farce, has to juggle his brilliantly coloured eggs in the air and not drop any of them during a sustained performance. Should he do so, the egg would be not on Kafka's face, but on his own.

PART FOUR

Formal Matters

11   Fact and Fiction

'My theatrical imagination is pretty limited,' wrote Bennett, introducing *The Wind in the Willows*. This is his self-deprecating voice, and it is not very accurate – his formal range is considerable. Very roughly, the plays divide between the realism of the television and film work and the non-realism of stage plays, but this simplistic division does absolutely no justice to their variety. The non-realist plays include *Forty Years On*, a multi-layered structure designed to hold together a string of revue-turn parodies. Schoolboys rehearse their end-of-term play about a couple who sit out the war in the basement of Claridge's Hotel. The couple's memories of twentieth-century history are dramatized as a series of literary parodies, making for plays within a play within a play. There is a new slant on traditional farce with *Habeas Corpus*, and also the intellectual, paradoxical farce with *Kafka's Dick*; *Enjoy*, a dark, surreal play owing much to the theatre of the absurd, like *The Old Crowd*; and, not least, the children's fantasy, *Wind in the Willows*.

The plays that one could call 'realist' include all the television northern plays, which are not all the same, ranging from the elegiac idyll of *A Day Out* to the pain of *Sunset Across the Bay* and *Rolling Home*. They also include the hope of *Me, I'm Afraid of Virginia Woolf* and the savage social satire of *The Old Country* and *A Private Function*. There are six plays about historical people. While *The Madness of King George* and *Prick Up your Ears* are realist, *Kafka's Dick* is often surreal farce and is like Stoppard's *Travesties* in the way it plays with ideas generated by putting historical characters into bizarre situations. *A Question of Attribution* is wittily and intricately structured, a game of intellectual parallels. *The Insurance Man* is a blend, not only of realism and a Kafka nightmare, but of history and fiction, while *An Englishman Abroad* is both a documentary reconstruction and a theatrical, self-reflexive piece.

This list leaves out the monologues, which are balanced between short story and play. It also omits the documentaries which become art: *The Lady in the Van*, an unclassifiable work which might be narrative if it did not include diary jottings, autobiography if the main character was not somebody other than Bennett, or biography, if only the writer knew more about his subject. It also excludes the television programmes, *Dinner at Noon* and *Portrait or Bust*, which mix autobiography and documentary. I do not want to imply that it is important to pigeon-hole and classify, but only to point out Bennett's originality, variety and subtlety.

Some of his most interesting experiments are the pieces which are on the borderline of fact and fiction. In one – *Dinner at Noon* – he records other, real people so that we can be certain that the voices we hear are not his own or his own invention; in another – *An Englishman Abroad* – fact is assimilated into Bennett's fictional creation.

At the end of *Portrait or Bust*, we see a self-portrait of Bennett, done while he was a student. 'I found', he comments, 'that the only thing I could paint was myself, so I stopped trying to paint.' He rejected self-centredness as too limiting, and opted instead for an interest in the outside world. The diaries in *Writing Home* show how acutely his eye and ear are turned outwards. They are full of observations of people and records of their speech. The voices range from Thora Hird's accomplished story-telling and Coral Browne's courageous joking, to the madwoman Rose in New York, an immigration officer at Heathrow and other complete strangers: 'In the market today: "Listen, there's nothing you can teach me about road-sweeping"' is one complete paragraph; at his uncle's funeral he notices a memorial plaque to Mr and Mrs Holdsworth, 'who lived opposite us in the Hallidays during the war and from whose nasturtium border we used to collect caterpillars'. Since he has selected these to record and then selected them again to publish, Bennett must relish the banal, ordinary and specific, and expect his readers to do so too. This is a version of what Auden identifies as the writer's task in 'Making, Knowing and Judging': '. . . praise all it can for being'. Similar little vignettes of real people's everyday lives get built into the artistic structure of *Dinner at Noon* and *Portrait or Bust*, and Bennett's delight in watching them becomes the viewer's. When, in *Portrait or Bust*, he recalls waiting as a child in Oddie's barber's shop on Shire Oak Street, the specificity and shared reference which he assumes, like the way he uses colloquial English, creates the confidential relationship he offers his audience.

In real life and among strangers, Bennett finds the same human oddity and crazy logic he transcribes into plays. 'He was a grand feller, your uncle,' says someone at his uncle's funeral. 'And he had beautiful handwriting.' He hears a six-year-old, when his mother telephones with news of his grandfather's death, say, 'Can I pretend that I don't know and you tell me all over again?' He comes across a woman who says, quite seriously, that her hobby is flirting with Japanese men, and he watches an elderly American woman in Moscow gamely adjusting to the harsher conditions of Russian life by piling meatballs and porridge directly on to her tray because she has not seen the pile of plates.

Some snapshots are expanded into little stories. Bennett watches a young couple argue and make up, and narrates it to a friend on the telephone as he watches. He and a friend watch men cruising in a park and make up a story about why one man is admired but not actually approached. In this, he is like his mother. He records in *Dinner at Noon*: 'My parents liked this side of hotel life . . . They'd station themselves on the sofa and watch what went on, other people leading their lives, and envying the accomplishment with which they led them. And, without realising it, my mother would make up stories about people . . .'. One can see how his observations might be transformed into characters as touching and funny, inviting as complex an emotional response as those in his plays. For example, in his account of the funeral of George Fenton's father, he describes his old army friends as 'good, solid, old-fashioned . . . never wavering, never doubting, and singing their hearts out . . . It's like *Forty Years On* – all that one loves and hates'. The dramatist in Bennett does not analyse what this 'all' is, allowing the figures he has put in front of us to represent it. No wonder that in *Enjoy*, *One Fine Day* and *Me, I'm Afraid of Virginia Woolf* he relates writer to voyeur.

Bennett has made two television programmes out of his habit of observing and recording people: *Portrait or Bust*, set in the Leeds Art Gallery, and *Dinner at Noon*, set in the Crown Hotel, Harrogate. The latter work, which is published in *Writing Home*, began as a documentary, a 'fly-on-the-wall' 'sociological study', and offers viewers a chance to be a voyeur along with Bennett. The camera picks up random groups of people and snippets of their conversations, offering them to viewers to enjoy, doing exactly what Bennett does with scenes from his diaries. But these television vignettes are embedded in Bennett's commentary, which is full of intimate recollections of his childhood and family, so that, as he says, the programme ends up having 'a lot more to do with me'. It is a curious mixture of documentary and autobiography, objectivity and subjectivity, and is set in a hotel, itself a blend of public and private space: 'American hotels are like station concourses or airport lounges . . . Here, with the sofas and the fire, we're still visibly related to the hall of the country house.'

The programme depends on the division between two different kinds of speech. There is Bennett's own voice, recalling the embarrassments and awkwardness of the past, his sense of being different from everyone else because money was short. It is conversational and confidential, and uses non-literary forms as he recalls childhood, italicized here: '*What it was* – when I was little my parents didn't have much money, and when we went into cafés *the drill was* for my *Mam and Dad* to order a pot of tea for two, and maybe a token cake, and my brother and *me* would be given sips of tea from their cup . . .'; '. . . while the rest of the clientele at The Waverley . . . would be *wiring into* "a little bit of plaice" or the "bit of something tasty" which the landlady had provided, the Bennett family would be having their usual slice of cold brisket and a tomato'. It is fully articulate and analytic: 'For years, hotels and restaurants were for me theatres of humiliation, and the business of eating in public every bit as fraught with risk and shame as taking one's clothes off.' Bennett speculates playfully, embroidering commonplace specifics with comic inventiveness, on how the road hauliers' wives, who are 'having a do' in the hotel, might have met their husbands: 'How at seventeen and soaked to the skin, one stood for hours at the Wakefield turn-off when suddenly Mr Right, ferrying a load of minced morsels from Rochdale to Penzance, slowed his juggernaut to a halt beside her . . .'

Then in contrast there are the recorded voices. These are not Bennett's, and they place us fully in the present. The camera lands us in the middle of things, and often leaves us puzzled about what is going on: '. . . she wouldn't tell me where it was she thought he might be, and I said, "You just pass this message on to him and tell him that" – I've had a bit of experience because I've gone through this – I said, "that you can't be haemorrhaging like that." He says, "You've got a very good friend . . ." ' I wish I could make out the story and relationships that lie behind this, but it has the untidiness, unspecified references and incompleteness of unedited conversation, as does the following: '. . . there'll come a time when Tracy needs special maintenance – probably on drainage'. There is a wide range of voices, from a five-year-old's to an old couple's; upper-class and not; a French Mayor, a lecturer on contraception, and a man rather touchingly rejoicing in being Chairman of the General Council of the Institution of Environmental Health Officers. Bennett often types them – 'Genteel Woman', 'Upper-class Man', 'Businessman', 'Timid Woman' – and they all get on with their concerns, either unaware of or unembarrassed by the camera and not at all concerned with the private embarrassments of Bennett's past or his observing eye in the present.

At the beginning, Bennett seems to state the programme's aim: 'I hope that's what the film's about – not class, which I don't like, but classes, types, which I do.' However, the final effect is more subtle than that. When Bennett summarizes at the end, he talks about feeling embarrassment and feeling at home, and about social and personal change: '. . . business people . . . are banishing class from hotels . . . They're at home in hotels . . . I envy them'; 'I wanted to find people who were as awkward as I used to be in these surroundings and show them it didn't matter. Only I didn't find them, and . . . everybody seems to know it doesn't matter.' The assumptions he had made were changed when he listened to the voices of strangers.

The counterpoint between his past memories and present self, between autobiography and documentary, implies even more. Bennett remains the observer, and has shaped the episodes he recorded into a pattern that has personal meaning for himself and can be felt by his audience. By doing this, Bennett is acting both as artist and dramatist. The programme is both a personal exploration and a record of the world: self in relation to the other. The dramatist makes these other voices serve a purpose which fictional voices could not, because they are real, and set the outside world in opposition to his own art. Bennett himself would have been perfectly capable of writing everything that the other voices say. What he gains from choosing not to do this is that he acknowledges a world elsewhere that is not invented or controlled by the dramatist, making him adjust his way of seeing. Perhaps, like us, Bennett would like explanations and wants to make up stories about these people, but in *Dinner at Noon*, he has acknowledged the interest of lives and concerns from which even his powers of shaping and invention are excluded.

If *The Lady in the Van* and *Dinner at Noon* stay on the factual side of the borderline that Bennett explores, *An Englishman Abroad* and *A Question of Attribution* turn real life into dramatic fiction. *A Question of Attribution* is more clearly fictional: that Blunt was known to have been a spy and yet still managed to keep his prestigious posts until he was eventually unmasked publicly is true, but this is only the roughest outline of the play. Not only are characters like Chubb fictional, but so is the long interview between Blunt and the Queen which is at the centre of the play. The shaping of the narrative is playful: it is built from two stories whose parallels are wittily and ingeniously developed. However, *An Englishman Abroad* sits on the borderline of fact and fiction. The television version of the play begins 'Although some incidents are imaginary . . . this is a true story. It happened to Coral Browne in 1958'. Coral Browne, at Bennett's invitation, played herself in the television version, although she was played by another actress in the stage version. Bennett welcomed Coral Browne's presence as turning the work back towards fact, even though he himself always refers to it as a play: it 'makes [the play] less fictional, but I think I like that.' Much of the achievement of the play depends on this delicate balance.

The audience does not know exactly what was invented and what was not. Coral Browne supplied the story: when the Shakespeare Memorial Company was playing *Hamlet* in Moscow, Burgess did indeed visit Michael Redgrave's dressing-room and was sick. Redgrave sent for Coral Browne, and Burgess invited her to his flat so that she could take his measurements and order suits and other clothing for him in England. Later, he wrote letters to thank her, and sent a cheque so she could treat herself to lunch. They listened to a record of Jack Buchanan singing, and Bennett learned from Coral Browne only just before filming started that she had almost married Buchanan.

These real events attracted Bennett's dramatic imagination, and what attracted him became the preoccupations around which the work is structured. The contrasts struck him: 'the elegant actress and the seedy exile'; 'Moscow drabness and London *luxe*'; her splendid fur coat and the camera dwelling on the dirty saucepan in Burgess's squalid kitchen. This developed into the main theme of the play: the sad, alien environment in which Burgess was trapped, and his inalienable Englishness, a topic which is central in much of Bennett's work. He also found this incongruous spectacle 'funny and sad', so that the story could be dramatized as a tragi-comedy, just the kind of material which suits Bennett's particular gifts, especially as he shares with Burgess the 'ironic attitude' and 'scepticism about one's heritage [that] are a part of that heritage'. In other ways too, Bennett found himself able to identify with Burgess: he 'puts some of [his] own sentiments into Burgess's mouth' when the character says, 'I can say . . . I love England. I can't say I love my country'. Bennett can understand a 'fastidious stepping-aside from patriotism' and, like Burgess in the play, is 'a glutton for gossip'. Bennett's empathy allows him to make the exploration of Burgess's character the emotional centre of the play.

Bennett added and changed some material in Coral Browne's story. He makes Burgess enter Coral's dressing-room rather than Michael Redgrave's, and so better focuses the play on her and Burgess. One remark attributed to Burgess in the play was actually made by someone else entirely: Burgess, as Bennett understands him, is like that. The pair of repulsive upper-class British diplomats, whose outrageous remarks pass so smoothly from one to the other that they speak with one voice, is so much a caricature comic duo that one would have guessed the invention, even if Bennett had not written in the preface that the Embassy scene was his. Presumably, Bennett also invented the scenes in which Coral does not appear: Burgess wanders alone in the huge spaces of the theatre foyers and corridors, sings a Church of England hymn in the lavatory, insults the cleaner and the stage doorkeeper with English public-schoolboy jokiness.

Of course, we do not know exactly what Bennett had to add to give the material neat and significant shape. We know that he is cautious about inventing coincidences that are too neat, in case it seems 'sentimental' or 'melodramatic', as he wrote about Coral's near-marriage to Buchanan, and the death of the lady in the van. The reality of the near-marriage allowed him to use the Jack Buchanan record to focus the play on a central theme. Both television and stage versions begin with a large picture of Stalin, over which we hear Buchanan singing. This, and the pair listening to the record, provide visual and auditory images of the tragi-comic split within Burgess between Russia and England, and of the contrasts between him and Coral. For Burgess, the record means 'home' and for Coral, it symbolizes a person. Structurally, it bridges the time gap in the scene in the flat.

But did Bennett invent Tolya? If not, did Tolya and Burgess really sing 'Take a pair of sparkling eyes', and did this give Bennett the cue to use other music, as quintessentially English as 'O God our help in ages past' and 'He remains an Englishman'? Did Coral really ask Burgess the questions we would all like to ask him in order to understand him, and did he answer them as he does in the play? Were his last words to her 'I do like it here. Don't tell anyone I don't'? Did she actually say anything like her big speech, delivering her verdict on him? Did the word, 'mum' recur so often, said by so many voices and, especially, did the tailor say 'Oh, madam. Mum is always the word here', or is this just Bennett inventing a recurring pattern of English upper-class discretion? It is possible that Coral was given a bath plug and lost her scarf, according to the way of the Moscow world, and it is likely that Burgess was under some kind of surveillance, but did a young policeman really follow him everywhere, constantly reminding him of the police state?

Above all, was the firm which refused to supply Burgess with pyjamas really Hungarian? Given that the events of the play took place in 1958, this coincidence looks like something else which Bennett might have found sentimental to invent. The scene is present in both versions of the play, but handled very differently in each. According to the preface to the television edition, Bennett disagreed with the director, John

Schlesinger, about what to make of the loaded reference, 'Hungarian'. Schlesinger thought that the audience in 1983 would not remember that the Russians had put down a Hungarian uprising in 1956, so he defused the line by passing over it quickly and giving the scene a jokey ending. Bennett regretted this, and when he remodelled the play for the stage in 1988, he made 'Hungarian' the climax of the scene, after which Coral muses – helpfully for the audience – ' "Oh," I said, and thinking of the tanks going into Budapest a year or two before, wished I hadn't made such a fuss.' It looks as though the Hungarian firm was not an invention, but it is the context, the contrasting settings, which produce two quite different value judgements and responses in the audience. In one, Burgess's siding with a brutal regime is challenged; in the other, it is not. How we see the character of Burgess alters accordingly.

Bennett has entered imaginatively into the character that Coral Browne met and invented a part for an actor to bring to life. The play explores possibilities about him, and is speculative and reflective about a person's inner life in a way that a documentary, a work of pure fact, could hardly be. Bennett has constructed a character dramatically, and has imagined how that character might behave when he is alone. He makes Burgess give some explanations: his secret life was a way of finding solitude. ('I believe this to be psychologically true', writes Bennett, indicating his speculation about Burgess's character.) He attributes to him other illuminating things said by others. He makes Coral ask him questions, and, whether they are invented or not, they need to be asked of him ('What do you miss most?'; 'What else is there?' 'I just want to be told why'). Bennett invents scenes that emphasize Burgess's Englishness and the alien society he is in, producing a tragic portrait of a man who has put himself into extreme isolation. In the play, Burgess invites a much fuller and more complex emotional response than Coral. The tragi-comic potential of the story attracted Bennett, but there is nothing sad about Coral, and though she is amusing, she is not absurd. Burgess is sad in his loneliness and isolation, and absurd in his contradictions: so unalterably one of a class and a nation that he has rejected and abandoned. Burgess, the character Bennett has had to create by fictional strategies, is much more moving, more interesting and more fully known than is the real life Coral Browne.

Another thing we cannot know is how accurately Coral remembered their conversation, or how closely Bennett transcribed her memories. Burgess 'made jokes . . .' – it is something else he has in common with Bennett – but how much of the play's wit and verbal quality belongs to Burgess and how much belongs to Bennett? Did Bennett coin 'You pissed in our soup and we drank it'; or 'No point in having a secret if you make a secret of it'; or the dazzling paradoxes, sad and funny at once: 'I know what I've done to be given him. But what has he done to be given me? Am I a reward or a punishment'? Burgess may have been entertaining, but did he go through life like this? The pleasure offered by such verbal play is characteristic of Bennett, though in this case we cannot know its origin for certain. This relish, this pleasure, is not a response which dark material invites in a documentary; only in fiction do darkness and pleasure coexist.

12   Film and Stage

A turning point in Bennett's career came in 1972, when his first television film, *A Day Out*, was made. The dramatist who had shown an almost entirely verbal talent in *Beyond the Fringe* and *Forty Years On* had obviously mastered the very different medium of television film. As he did so, he moved from fantasy to realism, from verbal play to minimal dialogue and from explicitness to obliqueness.

His own analysis of the differences between television film and stage play can be found in the preface to *The Writer in Disguise*. 'The difference between writing for stage and for television is almost an optical one', he writes. One of the sources of this visual difference is that television films are 'set in a variety of locations'. Language is also different in the two media. 'Language on the stage has to be slightly larger than life because it is being heard in a much larger space ... On television the playwright is conversing. In the theatre he is (even when conversing) addressing a meeting.' He continues, 'Plot counts for less on the television screen because one is seeing the characters at closer quarters than in the theatre. The shape and plot of a stage play count for more in consequence of the distance between the audience and the action.' The reasoning here is that television makes frequent use of close-up, and directs the attention of the audience to parts of the whole, whereas on stage the audience sees the whole picture all the time. That television is a more visual medium and stage a more verbal one usually means that television tends to be what Bennett calls 'naturalistic'; stage tends to be stylized in various ways.

It is possible to make a rough division of Bennett's work along these lines. Between 1972 (*A Day Out*) and 1982 (the five plays published as *Objects of Affection*) all the plays which are so characteristic of one side of Bennett's work were televised. It seems that he found television particularly suitable for a certain kind of play: the naturalistic drama about ordinary, disappointing northern life. This is not to say that Bennett's television work is restricted to plays of this kind. In 1979, Lindsay Anderson produced the strange and surreal *The Old Crowd* and after 1982, Bennett moved away from plays about northern life and wrote *An Englishman Abroad, The Insurance Man* and *Talking Heads*, all of which are for television. When Bennett writes for the theatre, he tends to produce plays that are non-realistic, like *Enjoy* or *Habeas Corpus*, highly verbal and generally full of wit and intellectual play, like *Forty Years On, A Question of Acquisition* and *Kafka's Dick*. But again, he has written for the stage naturalistic plays like *Getting On* and *The Old Country*.

Even in *Getting On*, where the play's naturalism should bring it nearer to television than most of his other stage plays, Bennett makes the qualities of stage drama work for him. Its central character is George Oliver, a middle-aged Labour MP whom Bennett describes as 'so self-absorbed that he remains blind to the fact that his wife is having an affair with the handyman, his mother-in-law is dying, his son is getting ready to leave home, his best friend thinks him a fool'. As the title suggests, it is a play about both ageing and making a career, set in a household typifying a particular sort of nostalgia. Polly, George's wife, obsessively buys things in junk shops, and George sees this as a kind of dishonesty: 'This isn't a house. It's a setting we've devised for our-selves . . . We're accomplices, Polly and me, with snake-hipped young men totting up back lanes in Grimthorpe and Featherstone . . . peering in through barricades of plants . . . for miners' widows gone a bit silly and willing to trade the polished artefacts of a life's history for a few quid . . . [objects] brought back . . . across the saddle bow of some chiffon-scarved Genghis Khan with a shop down Camden Passage and an eye for the coming thing'.

As this speech suggests, *Getting On* is Bennett's *Look Back in Anger* and George is his Jimmy Porter. Bennett uses the larger-than-life quality of stage writing, the way it addresses a meeting, to characterize George. It is particularly suitable that George is an MP, making his career from speaking in public, and we see him practising for an appearance on television. Like Jimmy, George expresses his cynical views and attacks the society of his time in long, eloquent speeches whose verbal flour-ishes and inventiveness make him entertaining. The speeches' very inventiveness also reveals how 'deeply misanthropic' George is: for example, his description of a chicken farm in terms of a concentration camp. It is an indication of his self-absorption that, like Jimmy, he is absorbed in his own rhetoric and his verbal style, one not at home on television.

Bennett has dealt with related material in a television play and a stage play several times. *Sunset Across the Bay* and *Enjoy* start with the same sort of characters and situation. *A Day Out* and *Forty Years On* both deal with nostalgia for the pastoral myths of Englishness. *The Insurance Man* and *Kafka's Dick* both deal with Kafka. In all these plays, the different formal qualities which the different media entail make him approach his material from very different angles.

To Bennett, television is the most patient form of drama, the one that can afford to linger longest on character and detail. On the other hand, in the preface to *The Madness of King George*, he writes of commercial film as 'drama at its most impatient'. Interestingly, he does not oppose television and commercial film to stage drama, but sees them as opposite ends of a scale which has stage in the middle. Television gave him the leeway for lingering in close-up on the lives of people who might otherwise be invisible. The language need not be larger than life, and this is suitable for characters whose culture may make them stoical or inarticulate. Instead, the close-up brings us nearer to characters who would not be able to bridge the theatre's stage–audience gap with language. The emphasis on location enables us to see the realities of their environments and the minutiae of their lives. The episodic nature of the plays and the lack of emphasis on plot are both true to the lack of significant events and consequent disappointment which Bennett sees as central in their lives. This makes the film dependent on the dramatist's ability to bring us close to the characters. The medium of the television film enables him to honour their lives by closely observing the small events which make life worth living. On the other hand, the stage play *Enjoy* develops the situation of *Sunset Across the Bay* into a surreal, black farce. Similarly, nostalgia for pre-1914 England is created naturalistically by visual reconstruction of locations in the virtually plotless *A Day Out*. Sympathetically observed characters do ordinary, random things which obliquely add up to a kind of experience. In a different way, *Forty Years On* is not concerned with character, though everyone has the gift of the gab. Consequently, it is explicit about what it is doing as it sends up nostalgia by the Chinese boxes of its elaborate structure, and by its parody of the literary canon. The northern world did not own this canon, or even have a literature of its own, and so could not be dealt with like this – or not until Bennett decided to parody his own northern plays in *Enjoy*.

Enjoy was written for the stage in 1980, eight years after *A Day Out* and two years before *Intensive Care*, the last of the northern plays. Here, the differences between stage and television are deliberately exploited, as the success of the play depends on its audience knowing what television has established as Bennett territory. It refuses the location shooting of the television plays, and can be acted in a simple empty space. (In 1995, the West Yorkshire Playhouse did an admirable plat-form performance on a bare stage.) At times, it moves deliberately and disconcertingly away from northern speech into parodying other lan-guage registers. The physical distance in the theatre encouraged the mannered, stylized plot with its multiple parallels (for example, the observers), creating critical distance as well. We cease to concentrate on the characters we observe in the environment, and concentrate instead on what the play is about: it invites analysis. One way of interpreting it is that this stage play is about writing the television plays.

It is not the only time this has happened in Bennett's related televi-sion and stage plays. He is quoted in a review in *The Times* as saying, 'In a sense, *Kafka's Dick* is about writing *The Insurance Man*.' In these plays, television allowed Bennett to write a play which places Kafka in his work environment, and suggests that much of what Kafka wrote was a 'naturalistic account of ordinary behaviour'. The stage play, with its wild fantasy, stylized structure and language bursting like a firework display into paradox and epigram, again invites analysis as it reflects on the bizarreness of writing about writers.

As well as the works in which similar material is fashioned to very different effect in plays for stage and television, Bennett's work includes some more obvious pairs: plays written for one medium and then adapted to another. Even though the plays are in a sense the 'same' works, the formal shift forced on the dramatist by the change of medium can result in different thematic emphasis.

When *An Englishman Abroad* was adapted for the stage, Bennett had to omit the many locations used in the film: the theatre, the hotel foyer, the splendid office and staircase of the British Embassy and, above all, the many outdoor shots of Moscow, including the last shot of Burgess, in his new clothes, crossing the bridge in snow. Instead, there is the empty space of the stage, and, consequently, Burgess's alien environment, the 'abroad' part of the title, is less developed and more oblique. With these scenes go the large cast of characters, so that the stage version is played by only five actors. Much information now has to be told rather than shown, so the structure is altered. The stage play retains only the central scene in Burgess's flat, albeit expanded, and the scenes with the tailor and pyjama-maker. These are sandwiched between monologues in which Coral and Burgess explain themselves and summarize events. They are addressed to the audience and larger than life in style, more elaborate and witty than would be possible on television. The monologue convention also allows Bennett to make the pyjama-maker's 'Hungarian' carry all its ironic implications, as

Coral can now remind the audience about the Russian invasion of Hungary.

The alterations that Bennett made to *An Englishman Abroad*, though considerable, are less radical than those he made to *The Madness of George III* when it was filmed as *The Madness of King George*. The alterations shift some of its central interests and emphases, while those of *An Englishman Abroad* remain the same. Even in the introductions to the play and the film texts one can see how differently Bennett reflects on them. In the introduction to the stage text he reminisces about his early training as a historian. He reflects on the dramatic handling of history in the play, and the particular problem of giving the audience enough information to understand the political crisis which the King's illness caused. Bennett indicates documentary sources and some of the ways he was forced to alter facts. He discusses how he handled historical figures and how he included in the play recent medical speculation about the King's illness. In other words, what he focuses on is the problem of dramatizing history.

In contrast, from his first draft of the film, he was concerned with visual matters – the setting and what it should be made to suggest: '. . . there should be a marked contrast between the state rooms . . . and . . . those tiny rooms and attics . . . where . . . most of the courtiers had to lodge . . . There should be a sense too that what happens to the King . . . is reflected in the topography of the castle . . . the contrast between what he seems and what he is [should be] echoed by [the contrast] between the state rooms and the attics'. Bennett's diary extracts about shooting the film also concentrate on locations. It is this introduction, not the introduction to the stage play, which states that he wanted to 'emphasize the unbuttoning that occurred once the King and Queen left the room' and 'the back parts of [the King's] personality'. Along with the emphasis on what locations can be made to suggest comes this more clearly defined thematic emphasis, a theme not touched on at all in the introduction to the play.

The Madness of George III opens with a bare stage and a huge flight of stairs that spans its entire width. The King, Queen and court come up the stairs from behind, 'so coming gradually into view', pause at the top and descend. It is a theatrical moment: a large space, suspense as we wait to see what will fill it; ways found to make human figures, who are not very large, fill it spectacularly. Not until that has been done does the spectacle focus on something particular, though not domestic: as the King reaches the bottom of the stairs, Margaret Nicholson attempts to stab him. The film, on the other hand, creates its initial suspense with close-up on a small detail: 'A hand (the sleeve military, the hand gloved) knocks tentatively on the worn wood.' We wonder what is behind the door; it opens and we see the court. The camera picks out domestic details like the Queen wiping a smut off a child's face; Braun polishing the crown with his elbow while the King is being robed; the King picking up his crying child. They then form a procession and move outside *en masse* around the cloisters of Westminster. From this opening on, Bennett exploits the film's ability to close up and pull back, taking in the large scale to emphasize the difference between private and public life.

It is easier to suggest family life by a few shots in a film than to have a small child in a theatre night after night, and the child Amelia appears again at the end of the film when the King is reunited with her. In the play, when the King is at his humiliating worst, he 'perhaps' shits himself: he clutches his dressing-gown behind him. In the film, his degradation is clearly visible, when the soiled and crumpled clothes are seen in close-up, and the King lowers his breeches and 'squats miserably'. Close-up dramatizes without dialogue the pathos of the King and Queen being separated when she runs beside his coach and sees him through the glass but can make no contact. Bennett points out that a little of the mad talk on which the play relied 'went a long way', so the camera's capacity to move around any number of scenes can show the King riding, interrupting a game of cricket and slashing thistles, providing a different way of dramatizing his restlessness and madness. While Bennett, in the play, was concerned to explain eighteenth-century politics and royal etiquette, the wider range of what can be shown in a film means that in this medium, eighteenth-century life is created visually. Therefore, the physical conditions of the time, public and private, are emphasized.

The impatience of film drama means that it has a different rhythm and emphasis to stage drama. Scenes tend to be much shorter in a film than in a play. For example, the dialogue for a scene between Warren, Pepys and Baker is only half a page of text in the film, but three pages in the play. The film glances briefly at the main material, but omits all the detail of the medical arrangements and the doctors' proposed 'treatments' of the King. In the play, the whole passage concentrates on the horrors of eighteenth-century medicine and the theme of misunderstanding illness is dwelt on at length, an interest which vanishes in the film, along with such running jokes as Thurlow's hypochondria and his habit of looking for free medical advice.

The climaxes of play and film are very differently handled. The emotional climax on the stage comes in the play-reading scene, when the King's sufferings find expression in Shakespeare's verse. This is then followed by eleven pages of text, which worried Bennett as anti-climactic. The film handles the climax much more conventionally and moves it to nearer the end. After the Shakespeare scene, the King sets off by coach to Westminster to prevent the Regency Bill being passed. Shots of the coach hurrying along are intercut with scenes of the parliamentary debate. It is like the conventions of old westerns: will the cavalry arrive in time? Of course, the King arrives before the vote and saves the situation, while the villainous Prince of Wales swoons in the background. This creates a problem about the Shakespeare scene. If the King is to respond rapidly to the emergency in person, the scene becomes an odd waste of time. As it loses relevance, the scene loses emotional power, and the climax shifts from the King's emotional agony and triumph to the more conventional victory of arriving in time to prevent a catastrophe. This is followed by only six more pages of text, including the cinematically conventional moments where the King's restoration is dramatized by showing his reunion with Amelia and the Queen.

Films need popular commercial success to recover the money invested in making them, and the title was changed from *The Madness of George III* to *The Madness of King George* in order to improve the film's chances of success in America. This is also likely to be why Bennett cut not only much about eighteenth-century medicine, but also much about English politics, which he had found difficulty in building into the play in the first place. Fox going abroad with Mrs Armistead vanishes, as do most of the political manoeuvrings of Pitt and the opposition, their use of committees, the effect on stock prices in the City, canvassing, the use of jobs and appointments to buy votes and the consequent importance of the King's failing to sign papers. Explanations are more basic in the film, as when Sheridan explains to the princes what Regency means or when Fox explains to them that MPs continue to support the King and Pitt because of 'pensions, places, bribes'. In the film, a few lines of explanation are all that is left of three exemplary scenes in which Sir Booby Skrymshir and Ramsden come seeking a 'place'.

For all these reasons, much of the historical context was cut from the film and the emphasis falls almost entirely on the King's personal experience. However, Bennett apparently felt that the plot then became rather thin: 'the plot needed thickening' is the reason he gives for additions to it. What he added was the story of the Prince of Wales and

Maria Fitzherbert. It helps with the problem of finding something for the opposition to do without involving anything needing historical knowledge. The story-line is used in a fairly conventional way when Thurlow discovers their secret marriage and uses his knowledge to blackmail the opposition and keep his job as Lord Chancellor. This issue is dealt with in much less melodramatic terms in the play, where Thurlow simply drifts into contact with them. The part of Greville was also expanded. That the hand knocking on the door during the opening shot is his and, as he makes his entrance, he sees the court for the first time – just as we do – makes him somebody with whom we identify. A little sub-plot is developed around him and Lady Pembroke. In the play, she is fifty; in the film, she is a beautiful young woman who takes notice of Greville. When the Queen needs to see the King during the regency crisis, she sends Lady Pembroke to Greville to seduce him into letting her see the King, an explanation that is not in the play. This increase in sexuality from the play not only boosts sales at the box office, but also makes the events more personalized and motivated in a more conventionally romantic or fictional way.

So the two ways in which the story is handled result in rather different emphases. In concentrating more completely on personalities, the film focuses attention on the theme of private and public life, the inner and outer self. For all that the plot is more conventionally handled, it has its own but different strength.

13   The Fissure

Bennett's two recurring landscapes and the way his work up to 1982 divides between stage and television show how central the split between North and South is to his imagination. In his plays, what Bennett calls the 'fissure' has been turned into the obliquities of art, but it is also stated straightforwardly in the semi-autobiographical television documentary, *Portrait or Bust*, and in *Writing Home*. Indeed, the latter title implies two perspectives: one writes home when one has left it but is in touch with it, and still has ties to it. The work collects writings – book reviews, diaries, obituaries, introductions to printed plays – drawn from a considerable period. It is interesting that when Bennett came to write an introduction for this retrospective semi-autobiography, he wrote an essay called 'In a Manner of Speaking', about the place in his life of provincial and metropolitan modes of speech.

In the book, he tells a story. Bennett's mother knew Mrs Fletcher, whose daughter, Valerie, married T. S. Eliot, and one day his mother was introduced to Eliot without having any idea who he was: 'T. S. Eliot and my mother shaking but never joining hands'. Bennett calls it 'a kind of parable'. It was literally true, but it also represents what happened inside him. The metropolitan Eliot represents, first and foremost, a kind of language – to his mother, speaking properly, which comes from 'stop[ping] on' at school and being educated, consequently having confidence; to Bennett, 'Art, Culture and Literature (all of them very much in the upper case)'. If his mother represents 'life (resolutely in the lower case)', then Bennett experiences a disconnection between life and literature as a split between two forms of language.

The depth of this gap ingrained in Bennett's imagination is made clear in another essay, 'The Treachery of Books'. In his childhood, life in Leeds meant picnics at the bus station; parents called Mam and Dad; Morecambe mud at the seaside; grass which was the 'wiry, sooty stuff that covered the Rec in Moorfield Road'. Life (upper case) in books meant picnics on a snowy tablecloth by a stream; a family with a Mummy and Daddy; dogs and a garden; at the seaside, exciting rock-pools with starfish and one could walk on 'sward' or pine-needles. This fissure between life and literature corresponded to the gap between north and south. Life (lower case) is rooted in specific places in Leeds and in a spoken northern idiom, while the novels which his mother enjoyed suggested that 'making good invariably [took] the form of going Down South'.

In *Portrait or Bust*, the National Portrait Gallery in London, which during the war sent its paintings to the 'remote and romantic haven' of caves in Wales, is contrasted with the Leeds gallery, which sent its paintings to Temple Newsam, distant by only a tuppeny ha'penny tram-ride that he had taken with his grandmother. 'From as early as I can remember', Bennett says during the programme, 'life, or at any rate life in Leeds, never quite came up to scratch.' He felt that he 'lived in the provinces and therefore on the sidelines' and valued the myth that Darnley's bed was in Temple Newsam as a reassurance that in 'this provincial city which seemed so utterly remote from any life I read about in books and which even the war had scarcely touched ... life hadn't always been elsewhere'. This is not simply the pose of a comic writer or the remembered fantasies of an imaginative child. There was a real painful feeling in his family of life being elsewhere, and this is shown in a sad story, told in *Writing Home*. Bennett's parents attempted to 'break out' by actually going 'Down South' in 1945 to live near Guildford, but were so unhappy that they returned to Leeds after less than a year: 'From time to time after this my mother's hands would be covered in terrible eczema ... "My hands have broken out again," she would say, and put it down to the wrong soap. But it was as if she was now caged in and this the only "breaking out" she was capable of.'

If Literature and Down South symbolized to Bennett places where life was to be found, it is hardly surprising that, as a young writer in *Beyond the Fringe* and *Forty Years On*, he used the language of literature and the south, and often exaggerated it and used it as parody. But even in 1963, when Bennett was appearing in *Beyond the Fringe* in New York, he wanted to try the possibilities of the other language. He added to the show his first piece in the language of the north, a monologue called 'The English Way of Death'. He does not now think it good, but says, 'I can see in it now the germ of the television plays I went on to write ten years later.'

In the first of the television plays, *A Day Out*, he once again tried to use his native northern idiom and his experience of provincial life. This time, it enormously enriched his resources as a writer to discover that the television screen could make central what was normally on the sidelines, that disappointed lives in Leeds could be given a dramatic life that came fully up to scratch and that, out of the fissure itself, a unique voice could come.

Bennett's diaries show his critical ear for phoney language and jargon, and so do his plays (for example, that of Graham's therapy group in *A Chip in the Sugar* and of Christian compassion in *Bed Among the Lentils*). He admits to 'an anxiety about sincerity' in 'In a Manner of Speaking', and relates the northern voice to 'being yourself'. But 'being yourself' is not straightforward, as he very well knows. George III acknowledges that when he says, 'I have remembered how to seem.' As he sits for his portrait in *Portrait or Bust* and as his self is turned into seeming, Bennett mumbles 'What they all say is be yourself . . .What they actually mean is imitate yourself.'

Anyone who enjoys Bennett's voice enjoys a language in which, metaphorically, his mother and T. S. Eliot shake hands. Even as Bennett tells the story of his mother meeting Eliot, the two voices co-exist in the narration:

> A few years later, when my dad had sold the shop but we were still living in Leeds, my mother came in one day and said, 'I ran into Mrs Fletcher down the road. She wasn't with Mr Fletcher; she was with another feller – tall, elderly, very refined-looking. She introduced me, and we passed the time of day.' And it wasn't until some time later that I realized that, without it being one of the most momentous encounters in western literature, my mother had met T. S. Eliot. I tried to explain to her the significance of the great poet, but without much success, *The Waste Land* not figuring very largely in Mam's scheme of things.
>
> 'The thing is,' I said finally, 'he won the Nobel prize.'
>
> 'Well,' she said, with that unerring grasp of inessentials which is the prerogative of mothers, 'I'm not surprised. It was a beautiful overcoat.'

Bennett sets the story in the north with 'my dad', but moves to the more southern 'my mother' as he starts the narrative. He transcribes his mother's voice so that the meeting is given from her perspective; it is separated from his own voice by quotation marks. In his own voice, Bennett uses the colloquial but standard form 'wasn't' to make the transition back from spoken northern to literary English, and shifts from 'my mother' to 'Mam' at a comic climax. By changing to northern English, Bennett puts himself into her camp and respects her scale of values. He signals that he does not side with the Establishment's view of itself. But he tells a story probably best appreciated by people who think *The Waste Land* important, uses some Latinate, literary vocabulary, and controls the syntax rhetorically to produce a climax ('T. S. Eliot'), a false climax ('without much success'), comic litotes ('not figuring very largely') and an anticlimactic descent into triviality ('Mam's scheme of things'). The voice he creates here absorbs and values both relaxed, natural speech and the art of the written language. That Bennett's prose is so animated and speakable owes much to how it has grown out of an idiom that is not primarily a written one. And how lucky this fusion is for a dramatist.

The difference between literature or fantasy and real life is one of Bennett's preoccupations. It has long been a source of comedy – *Don Quixote*, *Northanger Abbey*, *The Rape of the Lock* are examples – and Bennett often formally expresses this difference by comic shifts of register in which real life is figured by his northern idiom. In *Portrait or Bust*, he criticizes the sentimental art of Holman Hunt's *The Shadow of Death* by measuring it against the secret embarrassments of adolescence. Even the quotation from the liturgy belongs to the adolescent Bennett, who at sixteen was 'devoutly religious'. 'What always used to puzzle me as a child was that apart from the hair on his head Jesus . . . never had a stitch of hair anywhere else . . . God seemed to have sent his only-begotten son into the world without any hair under his arms. This rang a bell with me, though, because I was a late developer and at fifteen I was longing for puberty. And Jesus's pose here was exactly how I felt – crucified on the wallbars during PE, displaying to my much more hirsute classmates my still unsullied armpits.' The soft porn fantasies of the illustrator Matania get similar treatment, being made to stand the test of a child waiting at the barber's: 'The Destruction of Pompeii, brought about by heavy petting. Lots of thighs, and the occasional breast and plenty of floating draperies . . . And poring furtively over them as I waited for my short back and sides, I found them, aged eleven, immensely exciting.'

Bennett likes music hall, and in 'The English Way of Death', the first stage work in the northern voice, one can see him drawing on the northern tradition of music hall and radio comics, whose comedy comes from talking about life to an audience with whom they share a set of social assumptions and a set of references. The monologue's idiom is, not surprisingly, more exaggerated than that found in his later plays but, since Bennett sees it as having the 'germ' of them in it, it is worth asking what this seed is. Anything in common between *Beyond the Fringe* and *Sunset Across the Bay* must be something that is, in Bennett's imagination, fundamental to northernness. There is the respectability of the speaker who worries about scattering his aunt's ashes on the South Shore at Blackpool: 'the municipality won't want all them smuts blowing about there – it's a smokeless zone'. There is the emphasis on family ('our Florence', 'our Cora', 'my Uncle Wilfred') and the shared reference to specific places ('St James's [hospital]', 'the South Shore at Blackpool'). There is the emphasis on minor practicalities, like Mam in *Sunset Across the Bay* wondering where 'it' went from the lavatory in the coach: 'Then when you've got [the ashes], you've got to decide what you're going to do with them . . . They're always scattering ashes up on the golf course . . . it does the grass good.' There is the presence of age and death and the comic mismatch between them and small practical concerns: 'Mrs Passmore, she had her husband's put in an egg-timer. She says, "He's never done a stroke of work during his life; I shall right enjoy watching him now." ' There is the crazy logic of Bennett's own mother about Eliot's overcoat. There is the wide gap between the spoken idiom and the literary.

In the *Beyond the Fringe* monologue, the northern voice starts as a comic one. The piece is less funny when read in a non-northern voice and turned into a non-northern idiom. Perhaps there is something in it of the long-standing English comic tradition that non-standard language can be used to mock the naivety of the speakers, and perhaps this is why Bennett is uncomfortable about it. If this is true, when he returned to the north ten years later with *A Day Out*, any condescension had vanished. Bennett also writes in the postscript to *Beyond the Fringe*, 'The margins of humour were beginning to interest me too. I wanted to try my hand at material that was sad as well as funny . . . in my first stage play *Forty Years On* . . . I did try and combine comedy and nostalgia and found the result more satisfying than anything I'd done in *Beyond the Fringe*.' As has already been suggested, in *A Day Out* he did exactly the same in a northern play, his first – and successful – attempt to bridge the fissure between life and literature.

In *Writing Home*, Bennett remembers seeing musicians from the Yorkshire Symphony orchestra going home by tram with their instruments after a concert: 'It was a first lesson to me that art doesn't have much to do with appearances, and that ordinary middle-aged men in raincoats can be instruments of the sublime.' That conviction, his observant eye and ear turned outwards on the world, and his comic sense enable him to see ordinary life as full of interest, comedy and pain, which he could turn into art and in which he could find his main themes.

He uses his experience of the North/South divide, including his experience of language, to examine the experience of being English, especially the English way of making a lot of Englishmen feel marginal. His feeling that life was happening elsewhere goes into characters like Hopkins (*Me, I'm Afraid of Virginia Woolf*) and Midgley (*Intensive Care*). Eric (*The Old Country*), Joe Orton (*Prick Up your Ears*) and Coral Browne (*An Englishman Abroad*) are recurring characters whom Bennett himself describes as being marginalized by 'uncertainty about books', as his parents were. It is also part of the experience of being English to watch from the outside the people who are not on the margins. Bennett, going up to vote in Oxford, writes of the crowd there: 'It's like the theatre at Chichester, the same tall families, the same assurance of happiness and their place in the world. That is Theatre, this is University, both their birthright.' It is the same envy experienced by George in *Getting On*. As the first section of this book suggested, this social and geographical fissure formed Bennett's imaginative landscape.

Marginalized, people turn to a myth of something better. In *Portrait or Bust*, Bennett turns away from the guide who has just demolished the story that Darnley's bed is to be seen in Temple Newsam house, and walks sadly down one of those long corridors which are one of his landscapes of desolation in *Sunset Across the Bay* and *Intensive Care*: 'Heigh ho! Well, it was a myth that sustained me as a child anyway.' The myth of pastoral, northern and southern, recurs again and again in Bennett's plays, and northern plays like *Sunset Across the Bay*, *A Day Out* and *A Cream Cracker Under the Settee* yearn for a lost sense of community, a nostalgia that is savagely attacked in *Enjoy* and *A Private Function* and *Bed Among the Lentils*.

Bennett's own parents tried to make the myth real by moving south. In his own words, they tried to break out. Bennett generalizes this in his memorial address for Russell Harty: '. . . most people are prisoners in their lives and want releasing, even if it's only for a wave at a bus-stop'. His plays are constantly interested in people who are trapped and caged. This is clear in the limited lives of characters in the northern plays: Midgley, Hopkins, the Talking Heads, the Mams and Dads in *All Day on the Sands* and *Sunset Across the Bay*, who, like his parents, sought freedom and change by moving and whose hope collapsed. For them the small escape, like Phillip's (*One Fine Day*) few nights of camping away from home or Midgley's few hours with his nurse, is the triumph, the 'wave from the bus stop'. Their moments of release and freedom are limited and there is nowhere permanent to escape to. Ultimately, as *The Insurance Man* emphasizes, any refuge is temporary in the face of death, a reality constantly present in Bennett's plays, even

Habeas Corpus, the most wildly farcical of them. This sense of being caged is found not only in the northern plays. Bennett's upper-class spies are also trapped in the very Englishness they rejected: Burgess and Hilary in claustrophobic environments; Blunt by the intelligence services who throw him to the wolves at the end. George III breaks out in agony and madness. Franz in *The Insurance Man* finds out that the refuge he escapes to is his doom.

England does have regions other than London which have their own cultural identity. Someone from Yorkshire suggested to me that the county is not provincial in the same way that other areas of the country are, because it is so large and has its own structures and cultural history: he wrote that 'Yorkshire is the only region that is large and diverse and self-conscious enough to feel itself a sub-nation within the nation.' Perhaps this is something that Bennett feels also, for all his assumed diffidence. He has certainly been prepared to put much of his private childhood experience of northern life on to the national stage, and has found the confidence to fuse provincial and metropolitan in his dramatic art.

Chronology

1961: *Beyond the Fringe* (stage)
1966: *On the Margin* series (television)
1968: *Forty Years On* (stage)
1969: *Sing a Rude Song* (extra material for stage)
1971: *Getting On* (stage)
1972: *A Day Out* (television)
1973: *Habeas Corpus* (stage)
1975: *Sunset Across the Bay* (television)
1977: *A Little Outing* (television)
      The Old Country (stage)
1978: *A Visit from Miss Prothero* (television)
      Me, I'm Afraid of Virginia Woolf (television)
      Doris and Doreen (television)
1979: *The Old Crowd* (television)
      Afternoon Off (television)
      One Fine Day (television)
      All Day on the Sands (television)
1980: *Enjoy* (stage)
1982: *Intensive Care* (television)
      Objects of Affection (*Our Winnie, A Woman of No
      Importance, Rolling Home, Marks, Say Something Happened*)
      (television)
1983: *An Englishman Abroad* (television)
1984: *A Private Function* (film)
1986: *The Insurance Man* (television)
      Kafka's Dick (stage)
      Uncle Clarence (radio)
1987: *Prick Up Your Ears* (film)
      Talking Heads (television)
1988: *A Question of Attribution* (stage with *An Englishman Abroad*
      as *Single Spies*)
      Dinner at Noon (television documentary)
1990: *The Wind in the Willows* (stage)

1991: *The Madness of George III* (stage)
1994: *The Madness of King George* (film)
Writing Home (diaries, talks, essays, prefaces)
Portrait or Bust (television documentary)
1995: *The Abbey* (three television documentaries)

Bibliography

Alan Bennett

PLAYS

The Complete Beyond the Fringe, ed Wilmut, Mandarin, London, 1987.

Alan Bennett: Plays One (*Getting On, Habeas Corpus, Enjoy*), Faber, London, 1991.

The Old Country, Faber, London, 1978.

Office Suite (*Green Forms, A Visit from Miss Prothero*), Faber, London, 1981.

Objects of Affection and Other Plays for Television (*Our Winnie, A Woman of No Importance, Rolling Home, Marks, Say Something Happened, A Day Out, Intensive Care, An Englishman Abroad*), BBC Publications, London, 1982.

A Private Function, Faber, London, 1984.

The Writer in Disguise (*Me, I'm Afraid of Virginia Woolf, Afternoon Off, One Fine Day, All Day on the Sands, The Old Crowd*), Faber, London, 1985.

Two Kafka Plays (*Kafka's Dick, The Insurance Man*), Faber, London, 1987.

Prick Up Your Ears, Faber, London, 1987.

Talking Heads, BBC Publications, London, 1988.

Single Spies (*An Englishman Abroad, A Question of Attribution*), Faber, London, 1989.

The Wind in the Willows, Faber, London, 1991.

The Madness of George III, Faber, London, 1991.

The Madness of King George, Faber, London, 1995.

NON-FICTION

Writing Home, Faber, London, 1994 (revised with additional material, 1997).

Writing Home contains most of the essays referred to: 'The Lady in the Van', the diaries, and the transcript of *Dinner at Noon*.

The London Review of Books: the quotations are from February 1984
and April 1982.

Other Authors

There is very little critical commentary about Alan Bennett in print.
I have been grateful for reading the following:

Contemporary Dramatists, Saint James, London, 1988, has a useful
bibliography and an essay by Burton Kendle, pp. 44–6.

Contemporary Literary Criticism, vol. 45, Gale Research, Detroit,
1987, p. 54.

Ian Buruma: *The New York Review of Books*, February 1995, is an
illuminating essay.

Lindsay Anderson: the quotations are from his piece in *The Writer in
Disguise*, which discusses making *The Old Crowd*.

W. H. Auden: *The Dyer's Hand*, Faber, 1963, contains the two essays
cited.

The Times: 6 September 1986 is where the quoted review of *Kafka's
Dick* can be found.

OTHER TEXTS QUOTED

Kenneth Grahame: *The Wind in the Willows*, Dean, Methuen, London,
1991.

Rose Macaulay: *The Towers of Trebizond*, Fontana, London, 1962
(first published 1956).

Kenneth Morgan: *The People's Peace*, Oxford University Press, 1990.

George Perry: *Forever Ealing*, Pavilion Books, London, 1981.

David Thomson: *A Biographical Dictionary of Film*, Deutsch, London,
1994.

Passport to Pimlico (video).

Index

Page numbers in bold denote major section/chapter devoted to subject.